Praise for The B Words

"*The B Words* delivers an incredible blueprint to design your authentic life and become the person you are destined to be. From balance and babies to badasses and bravery, this book packs a punch about living with intention. I highly recommend this book for putting a stake in the ground about what you want out of life and aggressively pursuing your dreams."

—*Sharon Orlopp, Retired Global Chief Diversity Officer of Walmart*

"Tricia hits on all the issues that women face when navigating nontraditional roles in the workforce. Success is defined differently for everyone. *The B Words* is an empowering book that not only identifies the key issues facing women but provides strategies and stories that make it a practical tool. I highly recommend it to anyone looking to define success on their own terms."

—*Maria Guy, Senior Partner of GiANT Worldwide*

"Life as a woman in today's society is filled with expectations, many of which often seem unrealistic. But Tricia Kagerer is here to give readers the confidence they need to work toward self-defined success. *The B Words* offers thoughtful and professional guidance for women of all ages and walks of life."

—*Gail Warrior Suchy, Entrepreneur, Certified Health and Life Coach, and Nationally Recognized Speaker*

"A must-read for every male leader! Tricia Kagerer has written a book that highlights the challenges women face daily while focusing on what men and women can do together to bring about much-needed changes in the workplace. Tricia is candid about the difficult situations women experience—and rarely share. It's important that these experiences, catch-22 situations, and dilemmas are shared and discussed by men and women. When we don't know these stories, we accept the status quo, and things will never change. Put *The B Words* on your must-read list, and share it widely with your colleagues—especially men."

—*Jeffery Tobias Halter, Corporate Gender*
Strategist and President, YWOMEN

"*The B Words* is a collection of honest conversations that I wish I could have had with my younger self. They could have helped me avoid a lot of the frustration and emotional turmoil I felt during my more than twenty-year journey as an entrepreneur in the technology industry. Tricia Kagerer does a great job of addressing challenging conversations head on in an engaging way. She offers practical strategies and solutions for women navigating business careers. Furthermore, she addresses how the world is changing—and needs to continue to change—to truly benefit from the value of a diverse workforce."

—*Adrienne Palmer, Global Business*
Leader, Entrepreneur, and Speaker

"I wish I'd had this book twenty-five years ago. As a psychologist and entrepreneur often working in male-dominated spaces, I value so much the wisdom and practical advice Tricia shares here. As women in business, we all must navigate these B words in order to excel in our careers. *The B Words* is a great guide not only for women just starting out but also for those who have been in business for years."

—*Dr. Sally Spencer-Thomas, Author, Keynote*
Speaker, SallySpencerThomas.com

THE

B

WORDS

THE

WORDS

13 WORDS Every WOMAN
Must NAVIGATE for SUCCESS

Tricia Kagerer

BROWN BOOKS
PUBLISHING GROUP

The B Words
13 Words Every Woman Must Navigate for Success

Unless otherwise indicated, definitions of terms are taken from www.Merriam-Webster.com. Copyright © 2020 by Merriam-Webster, Inc.

Brown Books Publishing Group
Dallas, TX / New York, NY
www.BrownBooks.com
(972) 381-0009

A New Era in Publishing®

Publisher's Cataloging-In-Publication Data

Names: Kagerer, Tricia, author.
Title: The B words : 13 words every woman must
      navigate for success / Tricia Kagerer.
Description: Dallas, TX ; New York, NY : Brown Books Publishing Group, [2020]
Identifiers: ISBN 9781612543307
Subjects: LCSH: Women–Employment. I Career development. I Sex
      discrimination in employment. I Sex discrimination against women. I Success.
Classification: LCC HD6054 .K34 2020 I DDC 650.1082–dc23

ISBN 978-1-61254-330-7
LCCN 2020903856

Printed in the United States
10 9 8 7 6 5 4 3 2 1

For more information or to contact the author,
please go to www.TriciaKagerer.com.

To all the strong women who keep me grounded in my life, including Debbie Saad, Peggy Connorton, and Laura Gordon, and to my husband, Markus Kagerer.

Contents

Introduction

We are living in extremely challenging times in which both change and news are constant. The twenty-four-hour news cycle reveals unimaginable stories about successful, high-profile women enduring humiliating and degrading experiences for years. Although the industries have varied from news anchors, actors, and advertisers to farm workers and gymnasts, the stories are similar. Men—often intelligent, talented, and famous men like Matt Lauer or Harvey Weinstein—take advantage of women in a quid pro quo power play. The #MeToo movement has uncovered stories of abuse of power, sex scandals, and inequality. Social media provides the lens to focus on the desperate need for change. Where #MeToo pulled the cover back on the abuse, disparity, and power plays in the working world today, #TimesUp attempted to do something about it by creating dialogue, tools, outreach, and resources.

I am currently an executive vice president of risk management for a general contractor in Texas. Having worked in the construction industry—a man's world—for more than twenty years, I have experienced my fair share of crazy antics, biases, and comments that have left me scratching my head, wondering how I got into the industry in the first place. I have been able to create a successful career, negotiate a flexible schedule before such a thing became popular, and stay married for more than twenty-four years, with both of us working, traveling, and climbing the corporate ladder. It was not easy; it was stressful and exhilarating all at the same time. I am now at a place in my career where it is time to give back. If there is a glimpse of knowledge, encouragement, or favor that I can give to another woman who may face some of the challenges that I have, I hope to address it in this little book of "Bs."

This book follows the trajectory of a woman's life and career by identifying key B words that can propel her forward in creating the life she wants on her own terms. These words are challenges focused on helping you identify both what within yourself might be holding you back and external challenges, as well as strategies and best practices to help you plan your life. Be they internal or external, these challenges can blow women off course like grenades due to outdated, limiting beliefs and biases that still permeate our minds and the workplace culture of today. Identifying and exploring how to handle these real-life challenges can help you successfully navigate the minefields. We also explore living in your truth in order to form Bonds with other women, to embrace your inner Badass, and to engage men as partners to build Bridges. Your ability to make necessary changes along your journey to lay the groundwork for future woman leaders will allow you to earn the key ingredient to self-defined success: the Bravery badge. The information and stories that I have collected for this book include both secondary sources and primary sources in the form of anonymous personal interviews. The names have been changed except where noted to protect the privacy of these individuals.

Each chapter provides stories and sage advice, followed by breakthrough strategies on how to best handle unique challenges at various stages in a woman's life that impact her personal and career choices along the way. Whether you're just starting out in a new career opportunity, making the decision to have a family, or considering staying in or returning to the workforce, each stage brings opportunities to achieve self-defined success. *Self-defined success* is a simple concept based on helping you to recognize, sustain, and intentionally design your life in your own way and on your own terms for the benefit of yourself and others.

- **Beliefs:** What are the limiting beliefs lurking in your own mind that are holding you back? Limiting beliefs can change the course of your career, your family, and the quality of your life; only you have the power to change them. Together, we explore the concepts of inhibition and prohibition. I provide tools to identify the limiting beliefs that hold many women back and discuss how to change a limiting belief into an empowering one that can break longstanding negative patterns that keep you from achieving self-defined success.

- **Balance:** A mythical state that women set as a goal to achieve. It is like a gold standard. If a woman could balance family, personal, and professional obligations, then she would achieve nirvana. The problem is that life cannot be balanced. In this chapter, I explore why women need to reset the goal of balance to find peace. I challenge you to build a firm foundation by focusing on both your brain and your body, which will keep you upright.

- **Babes:** What is it like to enter the workplace as a young female? How can you prepare for and deal with unique situations? What should you do when your boss comes on to you? How can you develop a professional image? I provide best practices and advice from women who have been there on how to navigate sticky situations with grace and class.

- **Babies:** There comes a time in a woman's life to explore whether or not to get married, move in with a partner, or have children. Work is a gigantic influence on these life decisions, all of which can change, delay, and influence career choices. I focus on stories of real women who have made these decisions for themselves and illustrate how to create your authentic life above the noise of other people's views and opinions.

- **Budgets:** All women must manage their personal finances and speak the language of money at home and at work. Historically, society has conditioned women to believe that money decisions were out of their hands, leaving many ill-equipped to negotiate salaries, maintain budgets, and ultimately achieve financial savvy and independence. These are key to achieving self-defined success. I identify limiting beliefs around money that still exist today and provide resources and proven strategies that empower and liberate women both at home and at work.

- **Bankruptcy:** A woman's worst fear is being financially bankrupt. Women who never explore who they are and what they want out of life often find themselves emotionally bankrupt. I explore two limiting beliefs: poverty consciousness versus prosperity syndrome. Both extremes deal with money and life choices stemming from how women view the world. Furthermore, I suggest how to recognize and avoid the pitfalls of both extremes and provide a list of four characteristics of true prosperity.

- **Bias:** In the workplace, women are likely to encounter subtle forms of bias rather than overt discrimination. Unwarranted judgments are more difficult to spot because they are not obvious, yet studies show such bias is real and can derail careers. What are the subtle forms of bias, and how can you spot them? I share tools and techniques to identify unconscious prejudices in the workplace and steps that you can take to move toward change. I also explore solutions organizations should implement to identify and prevent unconscious bias in the workplace.

- **Bullies:** Bullying starts early in childhood and is alive and well in the workplace. It is real, painful, toxic, and of epidemic proportions. Is bullying behavior a sign of insecurity in both men and women, stemming from envy and power, resulting in fear? Or is it just to be expected in the workplace as a result of the worldview that winning comes at all costs—a take-no-prisoners philosophy at work? I provide recommendations on how to deal with workplace bullies and resources for starting an antibullying campaign at your own workplace. I also explore how to identify whether you are a bully and, if so, what you can do to change your behavior.

- **Bitches:** Women will be called "bitches" by both men and other women. This term holds different meanings both generationally and culturally. Sometimes it is good, and sometimes it is obviously meant to be hurtful. I explore various scenarios that lead to being called a bitch and address the inevitable implications of owning your bitch.

- **Bonds:** Forging relationships, connecting, and ultimately forming bonds are critical to both personal and career success. Women don't have to go it alone. Women network for different reasons and in different ways than men, and women benefit from recognizing those differences. I identify the purpose of networking and provide tactics and strategies to help women embrace the fine art of intentional networking.

- **Badasses:** What is more powerful than a woman who claims her truth and stands in her power? I share the recipe for achieving and ultimately embracing your own badass—knowing and accepting yourself so that you can make your own unique contribution to the world.

- **Bridges:** Women and men must work together to build bridges for the future. But how do we move forward, break down barriers to entry, and squash the zero-sum mentality that is widely displayed today? I provide stories of what it is like to be the only woman in the room and offer examples of the characteristics of the good guys who change the dynamics that historically have held women back. I provide resources and steps that people can take both personally and professionally to finally impact lasting change.

- **Bravery:** To live your own authentic life based on your own definition of success requires bravery. Many people go through life and never even think about what they want. I explore my own personal example of bravery and how I hope to change my corner of the world.

This book is for young women, midcareer women, and women nearing retirement. It is also for any woman who recognizes the need to get men engaged in a conversation to bring more women into every space of the workplace, including the boardroom.

My mother always told me to make a difference in my own little corner of the world. I hope this book is in your hands for that very reason and provides some guidance, awareness, and insight to make your world just a little better today.

Chapter 1
Self-Defined Success

> *Success is peace of mind which is a direct result of self-satisfaction in knowing you made the effort to do your best to become the best that you are capable of becoming.*
>
> —Coach John Wooden
> UCLA Basketball Coach
> and Expert on Leadership

Self:
1. The entire person of an individual.

Define:
1. To make distinct, clear, or detailed, especially to discover and set forth the meaning.

Success:
1. A favorable or desired outcome or result.

Before we begin our journey into the B words, we must explore the concept of *self-defined success.* I have struggled over the course of my lifetime with self-acceptance and self-worth. My most difficult struggles came from trying to live up to others' expectations and disregarding my own. I figured out that if I didn't know what I wanted my life to look like, then there would always be someone else standing at the ready to mold me into who they thought I should be. Living someone else's definition of success leads to misery; I realized that I was wasting my very own precious time here on earth. I understood that when I was pleasing family, friends, neighbors, and colleagues, I felt the emptiest, saddest, and loneliest. And as I got older, I realized I was not alone. I chose each B word as a check-in point to give women permission to explore and ultimately claim self-defined success.

Each and every woman has a different definition of success. The goal is to live an authentic life that is completely and uniquely your own. That requires sometimes messy, emotional journeys that may lead to a path never anticipated. Achieving self-defined success is neither linear nor easy, and not everyone in your sphere of influence—family, friends, and coworkers—will approve or understand. Self-defined success can be defined only by you. It can never be defined in monetary terms, and it will never be achieved by the acceptance of others. You must accept yourself. The only way to achieve self-defined success is to take the time to think about what in this life will bring you joy, satisfaction, and meaning. It requires stepping back and exploring yourself. Without knowing yourself, you can never truly lead yourself.[1] It also changes as you grow older; as a result, self-defined success is fluid and will look different at various stages and milestones in your life.

The Path to Change

For someone who is stuck in a dire situation or an abusive relationship or has money issues, an illness, or massive responsibilities, the idea of thinking about joy and meaning in life can feel trite. According to humanistic psychologist Abraham Maslow, we act in order to achieve certain needs.

Maslow first introduced his concept of a hierarchy of needs in his 1943 paper "A Dynamic Theory of Human Motivation" and his subsequent book *Motivation and Personality*.[2] This hierarchy suggests that people are motivated to fulfill basic needs before moving on to more advanced needs. It is a pyramid in which the lowest levels contain the most basic needs (food, water, sleep, and warmth) while the more complex needs (safety and security) are located on advanced levels. Considering some of the difficult situations that women find themselves in, the idea of thinking about creating a life of joy on your own terms and achieving self-defined success could be a luxury or a curse too painful to consider because the prospect seems too far away. The reality, though, is that until you give yourself permission to consider self-defined success, you may just stay stuck and accept the status quo. Self-defined success can be reached using eight key strategies:

1. **Maintain Gratitude:** Wherever you are today, whatever your situation—no matter how bleak—wake up in gratitude that you are here on this earth to live another day.

2. **Breathe:** Take a moment to breathe in the fresh morning air and give thanks for the morning and the day that lies ahead. Starting on a positive note and taking a moment to breathe will change the course of the day for the better, providing strength to move forward in a positive mindset.

3. **Explore the Possibility**: Stop and ask yourself what is important to you and whether the opportunities, pursuits, and challenges in your life line up with what you want your own success to look like.

4. **Dream Big:** Unleash the power of your imagination and create an image of what you would like to strive for in the future.

5. **Define Your Why:** Propel yourself forward by clarifying why you want to make a change.

6. **Write It Down:** Draw a picture. Save photos on your phone via Instagram. Create a vision board on Pinterest, or cut up magazines and make a poster board to look at every day. It

doesn't have to be fancy. It just needs to serve as a reminder of what is important to you on your journey.

7. **Work:** No one will ever achieve anything without moving toward a goal. Make a call. Connect with someone who can help. Read an article. Google your dream. Look people in the eye today and connect to see where and how you can explore one minute detail, one tiny step toward your dream.

8. **Chart Your Course:** It takes time; change may seem minuscule. It will also not be in a statistically straight line. You will have good days and bad days. By charting your course, you can check off items and keep track of the tiny changes that lead to progress. You will certainly be in a different place in six months than you are today. It may not be where you wanted or expected to be, but you will be in motion, and you will begin to feel something that no one can take away from you: self-respect. Self-respect for fighting the good fight and living in integrity on your journey to self-defined success.

These eight strategies require you to believe that you have the power to impact and change the circumstances of your life. Your belief system was set a long time ago, when you were a child, and is influenced by your family, culture, community, and experiences. It can be the single most empowering force in life. It can also be a detrimental hurdle that holds you stagnant. Let's tap into what society and your own internal voice have been saying to you and explore strategies for using your belief system on your journey to self-defined success.

> *You don't become what you want;*
> *you become what you believe.*
>
> —Oprah

Chapter 2
Beliefs

> *Beliefs are never neutral. They either propel you forward or hold you back.*
>
> —Marcia Wieder

Belief:
1. A state or habit of mind in which trust or confidence is placed in some person or thing.
2. Something that is accepted, considered to be true, or held as an opinion.
3. Conviction of the truth of some statement or the reality of some being or phenomenon, especially when based on examination of evidence.

Beliefs are the strongest influence that set the course of your life. As you grow toward adulthood, family, friends, religion, and social media continue to influence and ultimately establish your worldview. Once beliefs are formed, they become quite resistant to change. Some of your belief systems protect you and serve you well throughout your life. Because many of us never work to get to know ourselves, the worldviews we inherit from others become a part of who we are and how we make sense of the world. Beliefs are never neutral. They either move you forward or hold you back.

Limiting beliefs are those that hold you back or keep you repeating the same patterns in your life over and over. In spite of your innate desire to change, limiting beliefs can create no-win situations in which you go through life carrying around belief baggage. Even if you want to put it down or change, it feels too heavy, and you have no idea where to start. But what if there were the slightest possibility that your limiting belief was not true? What if it was holding you back from making changes in your life? Limiting beliefs impact both your personal and professional success.

Limiting Beliefs in Personal Life

Women tend to latch on to limiting beliefs and absorb them into their souls, creating years of unnecessary havoc and stress on their lives. If you have ever found yourself making the same mistakes over and over—dating the same type of guy and always getting hurt, failing at diets, or starting new projects only to give up after a few days—limiting beliefs may be the culprit.

Mary's Story

From an early age, Mary was the victim of a dysfunctional family. Mary's parents labeled her the stupid one of her siblings, which led to a cycle of self-abuse and disappointment that she never overcame in her lifetime. At the end of every school semester, Mary became despondent and sick. She never failed to have a stomachache the week before report cards came out. Mary remembers:

> Report card day was hell on earth. I would collect my report card from my teacher, go home, and present it to my mother, who chastised me and called me stupid. I was then grounded indefinitely from any and all activities until a few weeks would pass and she would forget. I believed with my entire being that I was indeed stupid, and I stoically and pathetically accepted my fate. My best friend sat back and

observed this pattern for years. One day she convinced me to do something different. She offered to tutor me. We studied together after school every day. My grades improved, and, for the first time, I felt a strange feeling of self-confidence as report card day approached. For the first time, I was not sick to my stomach when the teacher handed me the card revealing all As and Bs. I rushed home to present my report card to my mother, who responded, "Anyone can get As and Bs when you take the easiest classes at school. An A in tennis is a waste of time."

That was the end of that. Mary quit showing up to class and ultimately dropped out of high school. A few years later, she received her GED and went to various colleges here and there but never graduated. Every time she was close to completing her degree, an illness, money problem, or family emergency delayed the completion. Her life became infinitely more difficult, and she never really recovered from the lies her parents told her and she believed.

Limiting Beliefs in Business

Two limiting beliefs stemming from common myths have held women back for centuries and continue to stagnate progress.

Myth 1: Women's Work

Since the 1950s, women have served in administrative and caregiving jobs. Today, women continue to cluster in the lower-wage job sector, where they have minimal or nonexistent institutional support, scant benefits, and reduced opportunities to achieve wealth. Studies show that despite women's academic successes and legal victories, the top job for women in the United States is the same as it was in 1950: secretary / administrative assistant. It is followed closely by two other "maternal" jobs: teacher and nurse. Women compose the majority of low-service workers and make up more than 90 percent of paid domestic and health-care workers in the United States. These jobs are intensely emotionally demanding. Teachers, nurses, and administrative assistants all report a record-high rate of burnout, with emotional exhaustion as the primary reason.[3] Women who dare to enter better-paying, historically masculine jobs in fields like science, technology, astronomy, economics, finances, politics, firefighting, military, trucking, and construction report high levels of sexist hostility. Furthermore, a study from researchers at Cornell University found that the difference between the occupations and industries in which men and women work has become the single largest cause of the gender pay gap, accounting for more than half. In fact, another study shows that when women enter new fields in greater numbers, pay declines—for the very same jobs that more men were doing before.[4]

Historically, masculine work cultures in our society thrive on limiting beliefs that perpetuate the gender-pay problem and stagnate change, including:

- Women are caregivers and are best suited for this type of work.
- Women do not deserve equal pay.
- Women don't belong in what are considered masculine jobs.

Women in nontraditional leadership roles face subtle unconscious biases (chapter 8, "Bias") from male counterparts that are difficult to define but can derail a woman's career:

- She is emotional.
- She can be bitchy.
- She doesn't really fit in.

Myth 2: Women Can't Run Businesses

There are more than eleven million women-owned businesses in the US today, and 39 percent of all US businesses have women as majority owner, employing more than nine million people and generating more than $1.7 trillion in revenue.[5] The number of women-owned businesses grew 45 percent from 2007 to 2016—five times faster than the national average. In spite of the increase in women-owned businesses, women continue to face disproportionate challenges and entry barriers. Women are half as likely to start a business as men, accounting for only 4 percent of all business revenue.[6] Women have a difficult time securing adequate funding. Whether they're looking to secure a traditional bank loan or raise venture capital, they're considerably less likely to get the money they need (chapter 6, "Budgets"). The following is a list of limiting beliefs about women and business.

Women . . .

- don't understand finances and business.
- are not good with money.
- should not be in charge.
- dabble at side hustles and hobbies that are not real businesses.
- belong in marketing, human resources, sales, and communications.
- are only suited for teaching, nursing, and clerical jobs.
- do not have technical skills.
- are not good in analytic fields such as science, technology, engineering, and math.
- can't handle more senior leadership positions.
- are supposed to make less money than men.
- are not the primary source of income for a family, so their income is trivial.
- have working husbands who take care of them.

- are not supposed to work.
- should focus on being responsible for raising children, home care, and all caregiving family duties.
- make less money because they need more time away from the office to take care of their kids.
- are single moms because they failed in some way.
- are quieter than men and not meant to speak out.[7]

Because of these business barriers and universal setbacks like the wage gap, disproportionate caregiving rates, and stereotypes about women's interests and innate strength, it's tough to imagine how a business owned or managed by a woman could succeed.

My Limiting Beliefs Story: "Work Tricia" and "Mom Tricia" Collide

One of the highlights of my career was the opportunity to present at professional development conferences. It was a way to share innovative ideas and become recognized as an expert in my field. Every summer, I traveled to a national safety conference as a speaker. My parents came along and took care of my kids while I attended the conference. We turned each conference into a vacation.

In 2007, my mother suddenly passed away, leaving a large void in our lives. Instead of taking time to grieve, I continued to do what I did every year and accepted the opportunity to speak at the conference. I booked tickets for my kids and my father to come to Las Vegas, assuming Dad would help out like he always did. However, I did not realize he was as lost as I was without my mother and just did not have the bandwidth to help me watch the kids. As the event approached, I realized that I had very little time to practice my presentation. I wasn't too worried; I would practice when I arrived in Las Vegas.

After we checked in to the hotel, my kids began to immediately unpack their bathing suits, anxious to check out the lazy river at the hotel. As I was unpacking my work clothes, my kids were blowing up floating objects and searching for goggles. I made my way to the bathroom to change into "Work Tricia." I glanced over at my father, who looked completely horrified, as he declared loudly in his Bronx accent, "Where do you think you're going?"

I replied, "I'm going to work. You are taking the kids to the pool, right?"

He shook his head and said, "No! I'm not!"

It was like a slap in the face. I just assumed he was going to take care of the kids like he and my mom had done every other year. It never occurred to me that he wasn't up for the job. And so it began—two days where "Work Tricia" and "Good Mom" collided and imploded. I traded my business suit for my bathing suit and took the kids swimming for a few hours. Once they'd had enough of the outdoors, I brought everyone back upstairs to watch *SpongeBob* and take a break. While they relaxed, I threw on my business suit, jumped in a cab, and attended the conference, leaving my father in charge for a few precious hours while I worked. When I returned, the kids were wild, so I took them back to the pool and got them something to eat. Mrs. Doubtfire had nothing on me; I actually succumbed to wearing my bathing suit under my work clothes just to save time and sweat equity.

As the final day of our trip and my big presentation day approached, I was ready for all of it to be over. My father and my children were going to meet me at the airport. As I headed over to the conference dressed in my blue suit in the middle of June in Las Vegas, I began to sweat—not because of the heat but because I realized I had not looked at my presentation the entire trip. I was going into this completely unprepared, which was not something I ever did. I was always prepared.

I arrived at the conference room and met Brandon, the "tech guy." I quickly realized the microphone was up near a podium.

There was no other lavaliere microphone, which meant the only way I was going to see my slides was to turn my back on the audience each time I advanced the slide. I didn't even have a copy of the slides with me.

The room was filling up with people. It was too late to do anything about the problem, and fear and dread filled my soul. In addition, I had an unwelcome voice in my head. She is my inner critic. I call her Patsy. Patsy scolded me, "You are completely unprepared. Did you remember to pack the kids' bathing suits that were hanging up in the bathroom? You are a fraud. You have no business being here. Will Dad lose the kids on the way to the airport? You don't know what you are talking about, and all the people in this room know more than you. Will Dad get them something to eat? Are the Game Boys charged? If not, it's going to be a long flight. What were you thinking agreeing to speak? Loser! Who do you think you are?"

By the time I began my speech, I was holding on to the podium for dear life. I was literally clawing the sides with my fists, white knuckled. Someone introduced me, I heard polite clapping, and it was showtime. I started talking—well, babbling. I don't remember much of what I said, but I knew it was a disaster. The babbling progressed to droning on and on. People started to leave. I kept rambling. As I advanced each slide, I was just as surprised as the audience by the content that appeared behind me.

Finally, after a pathetic and painful effort to fake my way through the presentation, I gave up in defeat, ending the talk about fifteen minutes early. As everyone exited the room, I saw a man in a suit approaching me. For a split second, I thought, *Maybe it wasn't that bad? After all, someone has a question.*

It was Brandon, the tech guy, who proclaimed, "Wow, I bet you're glad that's over!"

I swore at that moment I would never speak in public again. Patsy, the critic voice in my head, confirmed what I believed. "You are a horrible presenter. You have nothing of value to offer. You wasted the audience's time and have no business ever again speaking at conferences." I nurtured and repeated these limiting beliefs in my head for two solid years until my cousin and I decided to write a book called *Wise Irish Women* and dedicate it to my mother. Once the writing was complete and the book was about to come out, I realized that if I wanted anyone to buy it, I would need to get over my public-speaking fears. I signed up for a speech class and started working on my presentation skills. It was there that I identified several limiting beliefs that were holding me back, including the belief that the audience always knew more than me and expected me to fail. I was an imposter, I thought; I didn't add value, and I wasn't really an expert. The truth is I could have talked for hours in Las Vegas without a slide or a PowerPoint because I lived and breathed my topic every day.

I replaced these limiting beliefs with new mantras that I repeated over and over. "The audience is my friend and wants me to be successful. They are excited to hear what I have to say and learn about my perspective. I am an expert, and I have value to offer. I work hard, do my research, and have experience and insight to support my point of view. I have earned the right to be there." This experience and shift in self-talk was life changing for me.

When *Wise Irish Women* came out, I did a series of book signings across the United States. Before I got on stage, I repeated my new mantras to myself.

Changing my limiting beliefs changed my life for the better. *Wise Irish Women* went on to sell thousands of copies, and I was actually on QVC. My career opportunities have expanded, and I spend a great deal of my time presenting to audiences all over the US. My father and kids made it to the airport that day in one piece, and we went on to have many more business trip vacations.

Breakthrough

For the most part, we inherit our first core set of beliefs. Our parents' beliefs become our own. My parents, the first generation in their families to go to college, were first-generation Americans born to Irish immigrants. My grandparents were all from Ireland and came through Ellis Island in the 1920s during the Depression. The limiting beliefs of my parents were twofold. First, money was always tight. Second, a college education was the ticket out of poverty. As a result, I adopted those beliefs. I believed money was always scarce and struggled with credit card debt. On the other hand, I believe to this day that education was my inheritance. I am a lifelong learner with a passion for finding out everything I can about the work I am doing. This has served me well both in my career and in my personal life. My belief system about money, on the other hand, was outdated and no longer the truth. It took me years to figure that out and ultimately change my worldview. We choose what we believe, every moment of every day. Our beliefs are our own opinions and judgments, but for some strange reason, we seem to forget that we can choose them.

Inhibition versus Prohibition[8]

We all have barriers that prevent us from breaking through to create the lives we want to live.

The first step toward breaking through what holds you back in any situation is to start asking yourself one critical question: Who says you can't . . .

- get promoted?
- start a family?
- apply for a better job?

- learn about finances?
- start a business?
- move to a new town, city, or country?
- marry your best friend?
- work while raising well-adjusted kids?
- take a vacation?
- write a book?
- speak at a conference?
- learn a new skill, sport, or language?

We have all kinds of reasons why we don't fulfill our potential, so our vision for our lives never becomes a reality. The answer stems from the limiting belief that something is holding us back. It comes in two forms.

Yourself: Inhibition

Inhibition occurs when your own voice in your head tells you that you can't do something.

Subconsciously or consciously, you inhibit yourself. Inhibition stems from several issues, including your own limiting beliefs about yourself. You don't know yourself fully, you carry wounds from past experiences, or you fear letting down the authority figures in your life. You may struggle with thoughts about not being good enough to earn or deserve certain things. Most of these are not true, but you believe them to be true.

What are the lies that float around in your head that keep you from moving forward? The next time you hear yourself saying, "I can't do that," pay attention. Before you decide that you can't, ask three simple questions:

- What prohibitions are you experiencing that stall your ability to move toward your vision?
- What inhibitions do you tell yourself are holding you back?

- Will you give these beliefs the power to stop you from achieving something that you could actually do?

What does it take to change a limiting belief to an empowering one? It takes willingness, choice practice, and faith. Be willing to choose a new belief and practice believing it by acting on it. Of course, the most essential time to practice believing your new belief is when you don't believe it.

Why would you ever choose a limiting belief if you knew it would hold you back? The number-one reason is fear. Humans fear the risks, the potential disappointment; failure and loss are deeply programmed. If you are not thinking yes, some part of you is already acting on no. Learn to manage your mind by noticing the choices that you are and are not making. Ask yourself, "Why am I doing this? What do I believe?"

Do You Suffer from Misdirected Faith?

Many people clutter their minds with the notion that they deserve to have bad things happen to them or that they cannot enjoy the good things because there is something bad inevitably waiting around the corner. This pattern is misdirected faith. Faith is the possibility that things will improve. The thought that you were meant to be here on this earth in this very moment is far more pleasant than the misdirected faith that you will be stuck in your circumstances, doomed forever to fail.

Someone Else: Prohibition

A prohibition is someone outside of ourselves telling us that we are not allowed to do something. It could be a boss, a spouse, friends, church, or family. Someone or something is prohibiting you from pursuing your vision and functioning at your best.

During the 1930s, the United States unsuccessfully banned the consumption of alcohol, making it illegal and dubbing the entire movement Prohibition. People were not allowed to drink without violating the law.

Throughout history, women have been prohibited from working or pursuing careers other than teaching and administrative work because it just wasn't done. There may not have been a law, per se, that actually prohibited it, but societal expectations and hiring practices made exploring other careers off limits for many.

Money

People often use money and time as excuses. When asked how much money a person needs to start a business, the answer is often, "I don't know! But I know I don't have enough." Time issues and constraints garner the same response. In our social media world and on-demand society, an hour can be wasted doing nothing of any substance or value. There is a new tracking mechanism on phones that tells you how much screen time you have used. Use it to determine just how much time you are watching other people live their lives while you sit back and accept the status quo.

Beliefs are never neutral. They either move you forward or hold you back. Limiting beliefs are internally controlled by your thoughts. Obstacles are external factors that can be addressed with strategies. The following process will help you move past limiting beliefs that are holding you back.

Here is a sample exercise to help you on your journey.

Step 1: Name and Claim Your Inner Critic

We all have a voice in our head. If you are thinking to yourself as you read this, *I don't have a voice in my head!*—that is her! That is the one. That is your inner critic, who will tell you all the reasons why you can't do something. I encourage you to name and claim her. If you ignore your inner critic, you will never be able to identify the thoughts that may be stifling your growth and holding you back. The following is a list of common thoughts that you may experience. Once you identify them, you can change them.

Limiting Beliefs That Women Often Experience

Limiting Belief	You don't understand finances and business.
Empowering Belief	I have a great handle on finance, and I have been successful in business.
Strategy	Sign up for an online class or attend a free seminar on personal finances. Make an appointment at your bank and talk to someone about resources they provide.

Limiting Belief	You're not good with money.
Empowering Belief	I am great with money at work. I need to get a better handle on personal finance.
Strategy	I will sign up for a money class by a certain date.

Limiting Belief	You don't belong in technical or heavy labor fields. You belong in marketing, human resources, teaching, nursing, and clerical jobs.
Empowering Belief	I belong in the field I am most drawn to, and I have the education and skill set to excel and perform.
Strategy	Research articles on women in the field you want to pursue. Call a woman who has made it in your field and ask her for advice and/ or coffee. Contact your community college and set up a meeting with a career advisor.

Limiting Belief	You run side hustles and hobby businesses—not real ones.
Empowering Belief	My business began as a hobby. I choose to keep it a hobby because it serves my current situation. When I am ready for it to be more, I have the skills, knowledge, and determination for it to become a relevant, lucrative business.
Strategy	Network and read articles and blogs on women who have turned a hobby business into a great success. Check out a book on how to write a business plan.

Limiting Belief	You make less money because you need more time away from the office to take care of your kids/family.
Empowering Belief	I make money easily and frequently. I am paid well for my services. I have the flexibility I need to take care of my family.
Strategy	Research opportunities in your field that provide flexibility. Make a list of skills/credentials that you need. Research companies that provide daycare, flexible schedules, etc.

Limiting Belief	You do not follow through on commitments.
Empowering Belief	I take commitments seriously and follow up in a timely manner.
Strategy	Make a list of current commitments and the steps you need to complete them. Scratch off the ones that no longer serve you. Let people know that you will not be completing those. Set a step-by-step action plan to complete each day.

Limiting Belief	You are not an expert. You don't have the skills/education.
Empowering Belief	I am an expert in my field and have earned the right to be here.
Strategy	Research options for continuing education. Review your benefits at your current employer and determine if they pay for continuing education. Sign up for a credential or a class.

Limiting Belief	You're not worth it.
Empowering Belief	I am worth it.
Strategy	Sit with a journal and ask your inner critic why she thinks you are not worth it. Write down the response.

Limiting Belief	You don't have time.
Empowering Belief	I devote time to my dreams and what is important.
Strategy	Determine one thing you can do to make more time. Do you watch TV at night? What about watching thirty minutes less? Look at the hours you spend on social media on your phone. Use that time to research opportunities toward your goal.

Limiting Belief	People will judge you.
Empowering Belief	I am not concerned what people think.
Strategy	Watch a documentary on someone you admire.

Limiting Belief	You're a procrastinator.
Empowering Belief	I am a high performer and get things done efficiently.
Strategy	Make a list. Buy a planner. Put activities in Outlook.

Limiting Belief	The people who are successful in this are out of your league.
Empowering Belief	There is no league. I am no better than anyone, and no one is better than me.
Strategy	Set up a call with a person you admire who you think is out of your league and ask her for a few minutes of her time. Prepare a list of questions about how she achieved her success.

Limiting Belief	You're too old/too young.
Empowering Belief	I am where I am meant to be today and now.
Strategy	Sign up for something that scares you, and do it.

Limiting Belief	People like you don't . . . (build businesses, become entrepreneurs, become successful).
Empowering Belief	I am special and can do anything I set my mind to.
Strategy	Journal about who in your life has told you this through their actions and words.

Limiting Belief	People won't take you seriously because you're (female, male, young, old, fat, thin).
Empowering Belief	People will take me seriously.
Strategy	Google search a person whom you admire who has a similar weight, age, etc. as you. What do you admire about that person? Write it in your journal.

Limiting Belief	You've tried it before and failed, so you'll fail if you try again.
Empowering Belief	I learn from my mistakes and move forward.
Strategy	Watch a baby learning to walk. They fall, and they get back up again. Recognize it as part of the human experience. It is how we learn.

Limiting Belief	You can't because you have kids. You can't because you . . .
Empowering Belief	I can do anything I set my mind to.
Strategy	Explore ways you can move toward your goal while you are with your kids or doing whatever else you feel is impeding you.

Limiting Belief	You will always avoid pursuing goals that matter to you.
Empowering Belief	I will always pursue goals that matter to me.
Strategy	Sit down for ten minutes and make a list of five goals that matter to you. If you don't know what truly matters, you can't get clear on your goals.

Limiting Belief	You can't ask for anything. You will be rejected.
Empowering Belief	I can ask for anything I need. The universe is open to help me.
Strategy	Write down two things you really want. Visualize what it will be like when you have them. Do this five minutes a day for a week.

Limiting Belief	The only way to success is to go to college, get a degree, and work your way up the corporate ladder.
Empowering Belief	The only way to success is to get clear on what matters most to me and set a plan of action to achieve it.
Strategy	In your journal, describe what success looks like to you.

Limiting Belief	You don't have enough money.
Empowering Belief	I have enough.
Strategy	Ask yourself the question, "How much money do I need to . . . ?" Then look at the money you have. If you have debt, make a list of all the debt you have.

Limiting Belief	You're too shy.
Empowering Belief	I am thoughtful and introspective.
Strategy	Shyness is often a way to describe introverted people. It is also a way to describe insecurity. Explore whether you are introverted or insecure. Take a free online test to determine your personality type at 5voices.com.

Limiting Belief	You don't know what you want.
Empowering Belief	I am clear on what I want.
Strategy	Make a list of five things you really want. Add a date next to each one.

Limiting Belief	Now is not the time.
Empowering Belief	Now is the time.
Strategy	There will never be a perfect time. What is one step I can take today to move forward in action toward my dream?[9]

Review your list, and distinguish which ones are limiting beliefs and which ones could possibly change if there were a strategy and a plan.

Step 2: Identify the Limiting Beliefs and Replace with Liberating Beliefs

Simply change the sentence from a negative one to a positive one.

Step 3: Create a Strategy and Face Fear

What are small steps you can take to move in the direction you want to go? If the empowering belief does not resonate with you yet, what can you do to get there? Do you need to take a class, set up a call or an interview, redo your resume, buy a book, do research, or jot down a plan of action? Once you identify your strategy, you can start moving in the direction needed to change the belief.

Finally, don't let fear be simply an obstacle. Fear is *f*alse *e*vidence *a*ppearing *r*eal. Wherever there is an obstacle such as fear, design a strategy to manage it.

- **Step 1:** Identify what you are afraid of.
- **Step 2:** Get into relationship with the specifics by taking action.
- **Step 3:** Get help or support where you need it.

Another limiting belief that has been a cause for concern over the last twenty years is the myth of balance. Balancing personal and professional lives is something women strive to achieve, yet equilibrium consistently slips out of reach. There have been times in my life when I have gotten pretty close to a balanced life, only to have it slip out of reach the moment after I acknowledged that I'd achieved balance. A balanced life is achievable. But is it sustainable? The next chapter will shed some light on the flawed expectations of a perfectly balanced life.

Chapter 3
Balance

Balance:
1. To poise or arrange in or as if in balance.
2. To bring into harmony or proportion.
3. To bring to a state or position of balance.

I spent many years of my life thinking that I would someday achieve a balanced life and finally be happy. On the journey to self-defined success, chasing a balanced life is like chasing a wave in the ocean. It will smack you down, then push you to shore, only to topple you over in a split second. I envisioned a balanced life as one where my marriage would be solid and my kids would be well mannered, kind, well adjusted, always respectful, and full of unconditional love for me. I would be able to tackle all of my work challenges with ease and grace, fully in control of my ever-changing emotions. As hard as I tried, my marriage was never perfect, and my kids were sometimes moody and mean. I sometimes lost my temper, yelling and screaming as I embraced the stereotype of a crazy redhead. Sometimes, I worked out and ate healthily, only to give it all up a few months later and have to start all over again. One of the beautiful things about age is realizing that life may never be balanced and that that is perfectly OK. Balance is too close to perfection, and humans are not perfect.

The definition of balance is "to poise or arrange in as if in balance," like "balancing a book on a head." Even the definition and example uses "as if," indicating the state is temporary.

Over the last twenty years, the idea of work-life balance has become the proverbial gold standard for women. Articles and books have been written about how we can have it all and create balance in our lives. While it is a noble goal to find balance between your personal and professional lives, I have learned the hard way that there is nothing easy about trying to achieve it. The closest I have come to balance is wobbly. If I were a piece of furniture—a stool—I would always be a wobbly one, with a matchbook placed under my foot to keep me steady.

Balance requires that the weight be evenly distributed. That is achievable when stacking a pallet or preparing a crane to pick up a load. Math can even be used to calculate the distribution. Unfortunately, there is nothing easy or calculable about a life. Whether a woman leaves the workforce and stays home, works remotely, or goes to the office for a full-time job does not matter. Life is always complicated. We never know what is waiting for us around the next corner.

My Unbalanced Life

In August 2017, I packed up my eighteen-year-old daughter and moved her into a dorm room. After all the years of juggling, scheduling, supporting, and second guessing my "Good Mom" status due to my deep Irish-Catholic propensity for guilt, it was over. She was moving out of our home and embarking on her own journey. I created bucket lists for all the things that would keep me busy when she left. The time had finally come. And for her entire freshman year, I did nothing to embark on the bucket list of hobbies that I had planned to do when she left. I never got in shape, lost weight, took up golf or yoga, or wrote a book. I never volunteered or fostered a dog. My bucket list grew cobwebs as I spent more time at the office or traveling for work. When Anneliese came home in May of 2018 for the summer, the reality that I had done nothing different with my time hit me.

While I was planning to start my new experiences, I was suddenly diagnosed with early stage melanoma. By the grace of God, I listened to my intuition, caught it early, and saved my life. I was traveling every week for work. During an annual physical, my doctor saw a small mole on the back of my leg. Being a freckle-faced Irish person, I thought nothing of it. My doctor said we should keep an eye on it for a year. I have a strong connection to my mother, who passed ten years ago. For about a month, I would hear her voice in the middle of the night when I was on business trips in hotels, reminding me to see a dermatologist. I finally made the appointment; the dermatologist looked at the mole suspiciously, saying, "We need to biopsy this." I was actually surprised a few days later when the nurse left a message for me to call back for results. Having had numerous moles removed, I knew that receiving a phone call was not good news. The nurse let me know that the biopsy had come back positive for melanoma. So began a series of medical appointments that quickly proceeded to surgery. I was very lucky. Melanoma is one of the fastest-spreading cancers, but since I listened to my mother's persistent voice from heaven, I am alive and well today.

Emotionally, my sudden cancer diagnosis was a wake-up call. I had been working many hours, traveling all the time. I did very little to take care of myself or to give back to others. I decided after the surgery that it was time to write another book. Thus began the journey of *The B Words*. I was doing research and writing down ideas in between work meetings and trips. While I was committed to the project, I had many starts and stops fueled by moments of self-doubt and limiting beliefs. (Chapter 2, "Beliefs.") I didn't really think that I had that much to say. Compared to what was going on in the #MeToo movement, I thought maybe my message was not very relevant.

Between August and November of 2018, I was doing interviews and continued to work on the book, full of doubt all the while.

I went for my annual mammogram in November, only to face yet another cancer scare. I was called in for a biopsy, which ultimately led to more surgery to rule out cancer. As I sat in the doctor's office weeks after the surgery to get the results on whether I had breast cancer or not, I decided that if it was cancer, then my book would go back on the shelf, and hopefully, when I was better, I would finish it one day. If it was not cancer and if God wanted me to write the book, then I would get started.

After an hour of waiting for my doctor, I became progressively more nervous and bored. I picked up the only magazine in the room, an outdated *Redbook* that was sitting on the windowsill. As I flipped through the magazine, the page opened to an article entitled "Women Don't Have to Take It Anymore." Reading through the article, I immediately recognized Dr. Gary Namie. I had interviewed him for the "Bullies" chapter (chapter 9) a week before the mammogram. There I sat with an article in my lap discussing the very challenges I was already writing about, the ones I had convinced myself were not important over the last six months. I was blown away; truly this was a sign from God that I needed to keep going. Just then, my doctor came in and gave me the good news. No cancer. I'm high risk, though, and I needed to make better choices, focus on my health, reduce my stress, and start exercising again. I dusted the cobwebs off my bucket list and started writing, exercising, and taking a long, hard look at what patterns of behavior no longer served me.

Breakthrough

Balance: The Illusion of Perfection

Here is the problem with balance. Balance is synonymous with perfection. It is never sustainable. Just like perfection, it is elusive. That does not mean that women should give up and stay in bed all day watching Netflix and eating ice cream. It does mean that the more we get to know ourselves and figure out what is really important to us, the more we can devote our precious time to what we really want to care about, who we choose to care about, and what we want to achieve.

An example came up during a conversation with a young woman who was a stay-at-home mom. After having been a businesswoman for ten years, when her baby was born, she and her partner decided she should stay home. She focused all her attention on her baby and creating a picture-perfect home. She lost the baby weight, decorated the house, cleaned, and cooked, all while nursing and having scheduled nap times. And she was miserable, jealous of the freedom her partner had to go out during the day and lonely from no longer working. After eight months, she decided to get some help with the baby and go back to work. The decision was the right one for her and her family.

> On the outside, I was the perfect stay-at-home mom, the mom I had always dreamed I would be. My days were full, and I seemed to be in complete balance and in control, but something was missing. Some people did not understand my decision to go back to work, thinking I was making my life more difficult. On the contrary, I had to give up the idea of perfection and do what I wanted to do. The house is a little messier, I buy canned baby food, and our lives are far from balanced, but I am happier, which means my family is happier.

Break the Illusion of Balance

1. Know yourself well enough to be honest with yourself. What exactly are you trying to achieve? Why? And for whom?

2. What are you afraid of? Ask yourself the hard questions about what you are afraid of losing. Is it an identity that no longer serves you?

3. Who are you trying to impress? Are you trying to live up to someone else's expectations? Are you attempting to save face because others will judge you for your decisions? Are you trying desperately to prove something to your boss, your family, your parents, and/or your friends and losing yourself in the process?

These are not easy questions to ask yourself. They will make you uncomfortable. Dealing with discomfort begins with realizing you can control your reaction to it. It starts with your breath.

Breathe for Your Brain

It seems obvious that humans need to breathe. Without breath, we die. Yet for most of my life, I never thought about the power of breathing. Simply focusing on my breath through meditation allowed me to calm my nerves, think, and control reactions to tough situations.

The day I was scheduled for my biopsy, I was a nervous wreck. I do not do well with needles. I'm the mom who felt nauseous, put on a strong face, and looked away each time my kids got a vaccination. I get "happy gas" when I get a cavity filled at the dentist. I'm basically a medical wimp. The biopsy was performed while I was wide awake, and nobody offered me happy gas. Local anesthesia meant that I would not be asleep when the doctor took the tissue sample. The doctor explained he would give me a local anesthetic and proceeded to insert a needle to collect the tissue samples. I'd prepared myself for needles, not expecting an electric carving knife fit for a Thanksgiving turkey to be hooked up to a vacuum and inserted into my right breast for more than twenty minutes while the doctor collected thirty-six samples of my flesh. The only thing I had to rely on to keep me from jumping off the table and running away was my breath. The room was tiny and sterile, a bright light shining over my head. No music, no sound other than the vacuum and the knife. I used the breathing techniques I had learned in meditation and yoga to stay calm during the procedure. "Belly, ribcage, chest; chest, ribcage, belly," repeated in my mind. I was raised Catholic, so I recited the Rosary for good measure. The Rosary is the Catholic version of meditation. I got through it—no fainting, no hysteria. I realized that breathing is the key to bravery.

Breathing Creates Calm

We are living in an age when people shift from computer to iPhone to TV to tablet with hardly a break. Scientific studies of the brain show that a fifteen-minute daily meditation vacation from the chaos of life is what your brain needs to destress, focus, and gain some healthy perspective. Like the muscles in your arms or abs, the parts of your brain you exercise the most grow the strongest. According to UCLA clinical psychiatrist Rebecca Gladding, MD, in her book *You Are Not Your Brain*, the moment you start meditating, you're activating areas of your brain that are often neglected, especially those tied to regions like the lateral prefrontal cortex, which manages anxiety, emotion, and fear. Within fifteen minutes, this shift in activity can lower your heart rate and calm your nervous system.[10]

Brain scans show two months of meditation can improve your brain's density of gray matter. According to research from Massachusetts General Hospital, the part of your brain called the hippocampus helps manage learning and memory as well as self-awareness. Studies have linked meditation to improved cognitive function and better emotional regulation, according to Sara Lazar, senior author of the Mass General study.[11] The same brain scans revealed that meditation causes a drop in gray matter density in the amygdala, the part of your brain that is activated when you become stressed out. Science shows the power of meditation. What are you waiting for? Download an app like Insight Timer, and get started now.

Become a Lifelong Learner

Breaking through the illusion of balance or perfection puts you on a path to becoming more comfortable with change. By getting to know yourself, you become more confident in how you react to things you can't control. When you give yourself permission to explore situations that get you out of balance, you commit to a richer, fuller life, and you are more open to experiences and education.

My grandmother Peggy Prendergast lived to be ninety-five years old; she brought life to every room she entered with her Irish brogue, which never left her in spite of her living in the United States for sixty-five years. With only a sixth-grade education, she left Ireland in 1928 to become a nanny in New York. She came here with only a suitcase and a few nickels to her name, but there was never a day that she ever considered herself poor. In spite of her lack of education, she was a lifelong learner. Every day, she read her papers and books. She was up to speed on world events, politics, and the stock market. She told me repeatedly, "Education is your inheritance. Your education will allow you to take care of yourself. What you do with it is up to you." Age has nothing to do with it. By becoming an expert in your field and embracing an attitude of being a lifelong learner, you challenge your brain and stay relevant. You are never too old to take a class, earn a designation, or take on a new endeavor. The technological world we live in today puts everything at your fingertips.

Now that I am in my fifties, I hear women my age or younger say, "I'm too old to go back to school. I'm too old to learn. I'm too old to change." That is the saddest way to live your life. Embracing lifelong learning and the wisdom that comes with age are the keys to achieving self-defined success.

In order to achieve self-defined success, women have to give up the notion that life will always be in balance and that we are in control. The reality of life itself is that sometimes we are not in control, and that is OK.

A time in my life when I felt the most out of balance was when I had graduated from college and started working as a "real professional." I call it the "babe" phase of life. Young, smart, ambitious, and ready to take on the world; sometimes it feels like the world may be ready to take you on. In the next chapter, I explore unique challenges women face when entering the workforce and provide sage advice as to how to navigate the waters.

Chapter 4
Babes

Babe:

1. Slang: girl, woman.
2. Slang: a person and especially a young woman who is sexually attractive.
3. A naïve inexperienced person—used especially in the phrase *babe in the woods.*

Over my years as the only woman in the room, I have realized that I had no one to ask for help or advice when I was younger and dealing with some tough workplace situations. If only I could have had the opportunity to connect with other women who'd had similar experiences!

Katrina was a young, intelligent woman who graduated with honors with a degree in risk management. She was excited to land her first career opportunity with an insurance brokerage firm. Her hard work paid off, and she obtained a position in a large international internship program.

Katrina could not wait to put her marketing skills, her networking abilities, and all the theory she'd learned in college to use in practical business situations in real life. The program was excellent, and she was learning valuable skills on a daily basis. Katrina was also facing some challenges as a young female that left her wondering how to navigate some potentially awkward career situations, such as:

- When addressing Katrina, some of the men used cutesy monikers such as "babe" or "kiddo." While the intention may have been innocent, the references presupposed mistaken familiarity and created discomfort. Katrina wondered what the meaning was behind these references. Were they innocent mistakes, though ones that could unintentionally negatively impact Katrina's credibility? Or were they intentional slights aimed at derailing her confidence?

- Katrina was warned by her older female friends to watch out for opportunities to advance for all the wrong reasons. Young women can find themselves wondering if a boss or a key client is interested in them inappropriately. Some single young women report wearing a wedding ring to ward off propositions or awkward dinner invitations. Katrina needed advice on best practices to avoid or mitigate the risk when responding to these situations.

- Katrina realized that first impressions matter and that wardrobe and confidence play a role in those impressions. Young women need to be aware of how they conduct themselves at work/social occasions, including how they speak and carry themselves, all of which has an impact on future career aspirations.

Katrina is not alone. Most young women entering the workplace deal with one or all of these issues. At the risk of sounding like a mother, I am going to cover some basic hard-and-fast best practices that have existed for years for a reason. They are helpful, important, and still valid today even if our world is very, very different.

Cutesy Monikers: Accept or Correct?

When encountering cutesy monikers such as "sweetheart," "babe," "honey," or "kiddo," women definitely have three distinct opinions on this issue.

Category 1: Let Me Call You Sweetheart!

Some women see no issue whatsoever with a male referring to them as honey, sweetheart, or kiddo. Whether it be a boss or a coworker, they believe it is just a habit, perhaps a cultural pattern that does not in any way detract from their professionalism or respect. Some women say that they like the attention and flattery. It is a sign of likeability and comfort. In fact, women of this mindset have commented, "If someone was raised saying 'babe' or 'sweetheart' to women and we have to police that wording as well as all the other issues we face in the workplace, when will it ever end?"

Category 2: Let Me Call You Sweetheart—Sometimes

Another perspective is that it is acceptable when a woman and man have developed a friendship over time and are both friends and colleagues. People develop close relationships over the years that span beyond the workplace by sharing personal experiences, knowledge, and camaraderie. In those instances, the familiarity is a natural progression, and the monikers are completely acceptable. It is up to the woman in question to discern when she is comfortable with it or not.

Category 3: Sweetheart?!
You Did Not Seriously Just Call Me That!

Consensus from professional and career experts says that calling someone "baby," "sweetheart," or "honey" is reminiscent of the "good ol' boy" network and has no place in business. Women who accept this behavior and let it happen are actually contributing to the problem, making lasting change difficult to achieve. They consider the monikers belittling and sexist and feel that they detract from a woman's credibility and respect and make women feel uncomfortable. Terms of endearment are demeaning and actually contribute to putting women lower in the pecking order. Some women report feeling like they were tricked into thinking they were seen by men as smart, formidable colleagues, yet when women allow men to subtly demean other women by using pet names, those women essentially hold all women back.

Where your opinion falls on this spectrum is not at issue. We have all had our own journey and formed opinions based on our upbringing. When one woman delights in being called sweetheart and another takes a hard line against it, it becomes confusing and difficult to create lasting change. However, based on the current political and cultural environment we are in, the future is category three. There are some things that need to evolve in the name of progress; being called cutesy names is one of them. However, novice young women often feel that they are powerless or that it would be ill advised to respond in any way to inappropriate comments from those with power within the company who view them as innocent "babes." This behavior, therefore, becomes accepted. Change in the workplace culture after this silence is unlikely and challenging. "Babes" need to speak out from the beginning and stand up for themselves as women to be respected and not demeaned.

Breakthrough

Courage

The key to women of any age being able to navigate these situations is courage. Women, especially young initiates, need to develop the courage to speak up for themselves in a nondefensive way and address issues head on. Author Brené Brown has spent her entire career studying courage; courage, she says, is achieved only when a person takes a risk and becomes vulnerable. Asking someone to stop doing something that makes you uncomfortable is naturally vulnerable. When that person is in a position of power over you and can impact your future career or your current financial situation, vulnerability increases exponentially.[12]

When I was in my twenties, an older man who worked for a vendor called me "Trish the Sexy Dish" every time and everywhere he saw me. One day, I walked into an executive meeting, and he said it again. After the meeting, I asked to speak with him privately. I said, "I know you think this is funny, and I know you don't mean any harm, but that nickname makes me uncomfortable, so please don't call me that anymore." He apologized and said it would never happen again, and he kept his word. To this day, he is still a colleague and a friend.

Liz Troccie Young, a business etiquette consultant with more than twenty years of experience in commercial real estate and development, explained:

> When you are uncomfortable with the way someone is addressing you and you want to change the situation, it requires action. I worked with a man who called me "Baby" in the workplace. I responded, "My name is Liz." He jokingly replied, "OK. Liz Baby," and I responded politely and professionally, "My last name isn't baby." That was the end of it. He did not call me that again.[13]

It seems easy to take action, but being smart and preventing potential career repercussions requires discernment and a plan. Consider the following before you immediately confront the situation.

- **Right Time, Right Place:** Did he just call you honey in front of a big client, a large group of people, or in a conference room full of male colleagues? Having the courage to speak up is one thing, but the right time and place is critical. While it is courageous to speak out in front of a group, it may also not be great for your career to correct a leader in front of everyone else. Think about how you would feel if you were called out in front of a large group. Have the conversation privately at another time.

- **Plan and Practice:** Articulating an issue concisely and accurately is critical to how the conversation will go. Less is more. Do not ramble and bring up other issues, resulting, in an "Oh, and while I'm at it . . ." conversation. Be concise, professional, and to the point. Practice so you are ready. Deliver with confidence.

- **Ask for Help:** It is tricky to figure out when to enlist help from a confidante, a mentor, or HR. You don't want to take things to extremes, but you also don't want to let things go when you see a pattern.

- **Review Your Company Policy:** When dealing with internal company relationships, it is important to understand the expectations of your organization. The basic standards should be outlined in your company policy. This is not to say that you need to run to the human resource department every time someone pays you a compliment or holds the door for you. Company policy is, however, your guidebook for behavior and expectations within your organization; familiarity and review will help you understand when and how to ask for guidance and help.

- **Find a Mentor:** Find a kind, trustworthy woman you can confide in, ask for advice, and connect with when you are unsure of how to deal with day-to-day situations. This is critical to your growth and success in any organization, especially as a young woman. Trusted relationships are made through networking and relationships (chapter 11, "Bonds").

- **Communicate with Peers:** Share your experiences with your peers so that you are forming connections and have a network of women you can carry with you and support throughout your career journey.

Looking for Love/Lust in the Workplace

The world of relationships and the rules of sex have changed a lot over the last fifty years. It used to be that women were lumped into two categories: marriage material or sluts. That is, thankfully, no longer the case. Women are now open to exploring their own sexuality, having kids with or without a husband, and actually reclaiming a say in their lives. Social media apps like Tinder make hooking up just another thing to check off the list on a Friday night. It seems like it could be the connection to something long term, but the idea of "What if?" may have been lost in the madness. Many people still hope for a long-term connection and a life partner. Work seems like a natural place to meet that partner. Yet there are still some very real situations that can derail your career when work and relationships intertwine. As a young woman entering the workplace, it is best to heed the warning and be aware of the consequences simple mistakes can have on your career.

Watch Out for Conditional Opportunities

Nicole is thirty-eight years old and has risen to the top of the technology industry, working as an executive for a *Fortune* 100 organization. As she looks back on her career, she recalls, "I can see just how many times my eagerness to move up in my career could have easily led to men attempting to take advantage of me. Perhaps it was my Hispanic mother's upbringing or just my ability to detect ulterior motives when I saw them, but I was able to dodge some traumatic experiences along my career ladder."

When Nicole was a nineteen-year-old bank teller, a prominent, well-known businessman in the community came to cash a check. She was excellent at small talk, and her polished customer service skills led to a longer conversation, followed by a leading question. The businessman said, "I think you are the kind of person my agency needs. You have excellent people skills and a great attitude. How would you like to come work for me? Let me take you to lunch and we can work out the details." Nicole was so excited and flattered that she immediately said yes. A few days later, they met for lunch.

Nicole recalls, "I received a 'handsy' greeting and immediately felt uncomfortable, and I could tell from his demeanor he was more interested in my body than my career. As we sat down at the table, he never once mentioned the job opportunity. Instead, he flirted and bragged about his money."

Finally, he declared, "I hope you see the opportunity for you here. Do you realize what a man like me could do for a young woman like you in life and in bed?"

Instead of slapping him across the face and bolting out of the room, Nicole sat there and politely finished her lunch. She replied, "You must be mistaken. I was interested in a job with your agency, but I am not interested in you in that way. Thank you." She never heard from him again.

I had a similar experience when I worked for a large manufacturing plant in Texas. I was twenty-four years old with a few years of experience. During my first year, I saved the company $1 million in insurance claims. This caught the owner's attention. Dan was a man in his late fifties—a widower who was known around town as a "playboy." He looked younger than his age. He was a smooth talker, showed up to work in golf shorts and T-shirts, and was the only man I ever knew at that time who wore a salt-and-pepper permed toupee! He drove a Corvette, and when he drove into the run-down old plant parking lot and pulled into the only reserved spot, which had his name on it, the energy in the entire building changed. Everyone perked up a bit, stood a little straighter, and moved a little faster. He was, in his own right, a celebrity.

I was invited to lunch with the CEO and the CFO. The CFO was an intelligent, considerate family man who always treated me with respect and kindness. I drove to the restaurant, both nervous and excited about having lunch with the executives. We discussed everything from my family to my future plans as the CEO gushed about how talented I was and the bright future I had ahead of me. He kept mentioning that I deserved a bonus for my hard work in solving his workers' compensation problem and saving him $1 million. He said, "I think you should receive a $10,000 bonus. What do you think about that?" I was making $22,000 a year, so I thought that would be awesome. Toward the end of the lunch, he invited me back to his house to "pick up the bonus check." I was about to agree to go inside so I could see the mansion that everyone raved about when I looked over at the CFO and saw that he was looking at me intensely. He slightly nodded his head no. We walked out to the parking lot, and the CEO said, "Follow me to my house. Or better yet, leave your car here."

I looked at my watch and replied, "I wish I could, but I have to get back to the plant. They are waiting for me!" I jumped in my car and drove back to work.

That night, I told my mother what had happened and asked her if she thought I would receive the bonus at work the next day. She laughed and said, "You are never going to that man's house, so you will never receive that bonus." She was right. I never received any bonus.

Breakthrough

The issues of power and propositions are difficult ones with no easy answers, especially for young women who are starting their careers. One thing is certain: the only person you can control is yourself. When faced with propositions, the following advice will help the situation.

- **Rely on Trusted Advisors for Judgment Calls:** Young women may sometimes go along with things they don't want to do—to say yes when they mean no. It may stem from immaturity or their upbringing, or it could be a sign of codependency issues. A trusted advisor can help you determine when you may be setting yourself up by being too trustworthy or gullible.

- **If It Seems Too Good to Be True, It Probably Is:** You have the gift of discernment and intuition. Intuition is that feeling in your gut that sets off a warning. Listen to it. Ask the tough questions before accepting a date or an offer. "Are you married? Is it appropriate for you to ask me since you are my boss?" It may be uncomfortable to ask, but it may save heartache in the long run.

- **Scope Out the Landscape:** Get to know people in your company, and find out which people you need to be wary of. They may already have a reputation; knowledge is power.

- **Set Boundaries:** Sometimes, gender becomes an issue when we make it an issue. Laura worked at a restaurant on the night shift. She had a boss who had a notorious reputation for flirtation. One night, she went into his office to take him the money from the register, and he put his arm around her on the way out.

With a stern face and a powerful voice, she declared, "No." From that day forward, he never tried anything like that. Self-assertion and adhering to your own set boundaries can result in earning respect.

You Only Get One Chance to Make a First Impression

Your mother was right: you really do get only one chance to make a first impression. Science shows that the human brain will judge information sequentially. According to Arthur Dobrin, a researcher in the science of first impressions, first impressions are related to a phenomenon called the halo effect, through which the perception of positive qualities in one area creates positive impressions in similar qualities.[14] Studies also show you have only seven seconds or fewer to exude trustworthiness and competence during a first meeting. The good news is that your first impression is something you can control. The way you carry yourself as well as your demeanor, choice of clothes, hair color, confidence, and attitude make a difference in your career. It says something about how you care about yourself and what you want the world to see every day.

- **Are You Heading to the Club after the Interview?** Over the years, I have seen women dressed in some outfits that would be amazing for a night out at the club, but not so amazing for an interview. High heels with spikes and sequins, low-cut blouses, and tight, short skirts—even minidresses and cowboy boots. All distract from the resume, leaving decision makers questioning a candidate's judgment and abilities. It is never a good idea to leave an interviewer with the impression that they would rather go out to the club with you than to work with you. If you are interviewing or going to a meeting with colleagues, err on the side of conservative. Less jewelry and cleavage is better in these situations. This advice is critical for young women.

- **Dress for the Occasion:** One annoying thing about men is that their wardrobe choices are easier to manage and are appropriate for almost any situation. They wear pants, shirt, shoes, and, from time to time, a jacket. Simple. Women have so many choices, colors, and patterns that it is difficult to know how to dress each morning. I would not change these conventions for the world because I love clothes and dressing for the day. But when working in nontraditional roles in the workplace, dressing right can be tricky, especially for "babes." One pet peeve is women who show up on construction sites in high heels or dresses with dangly earrings and lots of jewelry. I was in the middle of a catastrophic accident investigation on a project, managing OSHA, the police, the owner, and a slew of witnesses, media, and the public, when the claims adjuster showed up. She was supposed to be there to help with the investigation and gather the facts. She was wearing a flowing polka dot dress and heels. We were in the middle of a dirt field during a dust storm, and the wind was blowing her dress. She was more concerned about holding her dress than she was about the terrible incident. She wanted to sit in the jobsite trailer, but the project was so new that there was not one available. I finally agreed to take her photos, collect all the information she needed, and meet her at her hotel lobby the next morning. I called the carrier and advised them about the need to send people wearing the proper attire to the worksite. Even if she was an excellent resource, her wardrobe choice made her an additional liability during a crisis.

- **Wear Your Uniform with Pride:** In construction, make sure you have the right boots, a pair of jeans, and your personal protective equipment (PPE) with you at all times. You may need to change from business attire to worksite attire during the day, but if you don't have it with you, you will be a distraction or, worse, a problem to deal with. If the site requires PPE, follow all the rules, even if you are just visiting. This gear is for your protection. I have actually seen women in manufacturing using earplugs as a hair tie. Not a good look. Yoga pants are for yoga, a brisk walk, or a workout. Unless you work at Lululemon, they are not for the office, even on casual Friday.

Breakthrough

Your Appearance Matters

Clothes matter; for young women, fashion choices can be tricky. Your physical appearance and how you dress impact how people make snap judgments on your character and abilities. You can also ensure that you look clean and neat (tuck in your top, keep your hair styled, and, if it applies to you, keep makeup simple) and that you are dressed appropriately for the work or social situation.

Things have definitely relaxed over the last thirty years, and many companies have thrown out the dress code. And yet people still notice. Why leave it to chance and take a risk? Have a few classic pieces in your wardrobe, and wear them when you need to look polished and focused. Make sure they fit. Why spend all that time, money, and commitment learning your craft or pursuing an education only to limit your opportunities because of something as simple as clothing?

Every occupation and office will have its own dress code, and there is no single way to dress for all occasions. It's up to you to crack that dress code; one simple way you can do so is through imitation. Look at the appearance of well-dressed employees and leaders in your field. Are they wearing suit jackets or dresses, or is it a more casual work environment? Read your company's dress code policy, and follow it. Be aware of your company's policies regarding tattoos and piercings, and follow them. If it is a no-tattoo office, cover yours up.

Also, it never hurts to be prepared for casual and dress scenarios. If you can, have some dress shoes, a dress shirt or blouse, and a dress jacket at work in case you have to dress up for an unexpected meeting, presentation, or event.

Bring on the Polish

Your reputation and professional brand are important; they will follow you for the rest of your life. In fact, what may take you a lifetime to create can be shattered in a minute. The following are some best practices that can help you develop and maintain your brand and reputation for the rest of your life.

Carry Yourself as Though You Know Where You Are Going

My daughter had a serious medical condition that was discovered at thirteen years of age. She was diagnosed with scoliosis; to prevent having to have invasive surgery, she wore a full body brace for more than a year. She wore it twenty-three hours a day, taking it off only to exercise and shower. The brace restricted her movement, so she could not bend down to pick up anything off of the floor. She sat up straight in class and was the tallest of the girls in choir practice. Soon people began to notice her beautiful posture, which boosted her confidence. While wearing the brace was a very emotional experience for her, it resulted in two great benefits. First, she never needed to have surgery. Second, to this day, she has excellent posture. Walking with your head held high, with your shoulders back, and with a purpose is one way to carry yourself with confidence.

Look People in the Eye

It seems easy and obvious to look people in the eye. For some, however, it does not come naturally and requires practice. Eye contact is extremely important in building trust, exuding confidence, and making human connections. There are four reasons eye contact is so important:

1. **Our Eyes Were Made to Connect:** Eyes are free-moving orbs lodged in an otherwise stationary face. Humans are the only primates whose irises and pupils float on a bright white canvas. No other primates have whites in the eyes that can be readily seen. Eyes are required to see, and eye contact is required to actually see another human.

2. **Our Eyes Reveal Our Thoughts and Feelings:** You've probably heard the old expression, "The eyes are the window to the soul." While that may not be literally true, they do reveal a great deal about what we're really thinking and feeling from moment to moment. We're attracted to people who have "kind eyes" and eyes that "sparkle" and "glow." We describe someone with energy and eagerness as "bright eyed." People who are bored or disinterested have eyes that are "glazed over." The human propensity to look to someone's eyes in order to decipher what they're thinking starts very early in life. At around nine to eighteen months old, infants will begin to look to their parents' eyes to figure out what they're trying to convey. Eye contact is a form of simultaneous communication. You don't have to take turns expressing yourselves as you do with talking. If you have ever had a mini conversation across the room with your best friend using only your eyes, you know how this works.

3. **Eye Contact Shows Attention:** Despite the fact that, in our social media world, we're more connected than ever, we are starved for attention. Humans require human interaction. Eye contact provides confirmation to another person that you are interested and engaged. In today's world, it is so common for people to glance at their phones during a conversation, which can be interpreted as disinterest or even disrespect. The ability to maintain eye contact is an especially powerful gift—the gift of your time and undivided attention. These qualities are ingredients needed to build long-lasting, trusting relationships.

4. **Eye Contact Creates a Bond:** The human brain has "mirror neurons" that are activated when we observe another human performing a task or feeling an emotion. Eye contact creates mirror neurons through which we really feel what someone else is feeling, creating empathy and a strong bond.[15]

Learn the Art of the Handshake

A handshake is more than just a greeting. It is also a message about your personality and confidence level. In business, a handshake is an important tool in making the right first impression. The following is a guideline for how to shake hands in the United States:

1. **Introduce Yourself:** Immediately before you begin to extend your hand, start to introduce yourself. Say, "Hello, my name is . . ."

2. **Two-Pump Shake:** A firm two-pump handshake is brief and to the point. It is a short sound bite, not a long advertisement.

3. **Elbow Engaged:** Shake from the elbow, not the shoulder. You are not arm wrestling. But you are not a noodle, either. A firm shake from the elbow is just the right strength.

4. **Grip:** Your grip should be firm. You do not want to present a wimpy hand or a vice grip. The strength with which you would turn a doorknob is the way to go. Your fingers are attached to your hand, so offer your whole hand, not just your fingers.

5. **One Hand:** Use only your right hand. Don't cover the hand with your other hand.

6. **Three Seconds:** No need for the handshake to go on longer than three to four seconds. Let go after the verbal introduction is complete.

7. **Sweat Happens:** If you shake a sweaty hand, do not wipe the sweat on your pants or get out a tissue immediately. It is rude and may embarrass the other person.

Express Yourself Clearly and Confidently

Back in the day, I had a terrible habit of saying "you know" in the middle of my sentences. When I went to speech class, it was brought to my attention. I was able to fix this annoying habit, but I soon noticed that I'd started saying "um" in its place. Notice your speech patterns, and work on tone, pitch, and intonation.

Some things to pay attention to include:

1. Do you use filler words such as "like," "you know," "I mean," "right," or "um" as a habit?
2. When presenting an idea, do you say things like, "This may be a dumb idea, but . . ."?

3. Are your thoughts or ideas scattered? Do you find yourself talking in circles?
4. Do you have a habit of overexplaining yourself?

All of these habits take away from your polished, professional image and can derail your credibility at work. The key to solving these patterns is awareness and practice. Once you are aware of a speech pattern, you can do something about it.

Listen to Your Voice

Years ago, I had the opportunity to attend a workshop by celebrity speech coach Arthur Samuel Joseph. He is the author of the book *Vocal Power: Harnessing the Power Within.*[16] Your voice is an important part of your image and can enhance or detract from the message you want to send about yourself.

It is also a big part of your identity and can make statements about your credibility and intelligence, especially if you are a babe starting in a new career. I have a talent of being able to imitate accents pretty easily. Even though I grew up in Texas, I never had a Texan accent until I moved away to Denver to go to college. For some reason, everyone thought I should have a Texan twang. So, in an effort to develop my new college identity, I started talking with one. When I went home for Thanksgiving, my mother and father, who grew up in the Bronx, admonished me, "Stop that Texas accent stuff. It's annoying."

Your voice makes statements about you to the world and on the job. You can train your voice to sound calm, friendly, and professional. Awareness of your habits is the first step to polishing up any distractions.

Master Small Talk

One of my mentors gave me this great piece of advice: read the *Wall Street Journal* every morning, and read the front page of the newspaper of the city you are visiting before your meeting. That way, you can make conversation about current events that are specific to your client's home or city. You will also become well informed about the world and business.

Successfully navigating a career in my twenties and coming out the other end relatively unscathed was a big accomplishment for me. Just as I was becoming confident and developing a solid skill set and resume that would bring more career challenges, I decided to give it all up, get married, move to a foreign country, and start a family. Once again, my need for balance, perfection, and control was under self-attack. Everyone thought I had lost my mind. Yet it was a deeply personal decision that came with lots of challenges, stress, and sometimes heartache. And it was all worth it in the end.

Next I will explore the decision to have babies, a choice every woman will make at one point in life or another. Whether to marry, stay single, have a child, or start a family impacts every aspect of a woman's life, including her body, faith, education, and career. It should be entirely up to her. But is it?

Chapter 5
Babies

Baby:
1. An extremely young child, especially: infant.
2. Something that is one's special responsibility, achievement, or interest.

This chapter is focused on all aspects of family, not just children. I will explore stories from women—married, single, divorced—with kids and without. There comes a time in every woman's life to decide whether to start a family. Women, at one point or another, ponder the prospect of reproduction. Sometimes, the decision is made by fate or an unplanned surprise. Other times, women create a life plan, deciding when to start a family based on their career aspirations and timing. Some women decide not to have a traditional family of their own at all. The best thing about living in our evolved world today is that the stigma of these decisions and judgments is changing, and people are free to express themselves and live the way they choose more now than ever before. The decision to have a family is personal, private, and life changing, and it is one that will have a lasting impact on a woman's career. Having children changes the dynamic at work. Work really should have nothing to do with the choice to reproduce. Yet there is probably no other event in life that impacts a woman's career more than starting a family.

While we are far move evolved than we were twenty years ago, women's choices about family are still complicated by a lot of baggage, false doctrines, and judgments. There are also financial implications and social stigmas that fall squarely on a woman's shoulders. The following stories of women who have navigated their own paths to self-defined success provide a realistic view of challenging considerations and insight.

Young and Single, Hoping to Have a Family Someday

Lena is a twenty-six-year-old project engineer who would love to meet her life partner, settle down, and have kids. She is concerned that her career aspirations would never accommodate children and family.

> I work more than eighty hours a week, and the expectations are extremely high. When I become a project manager, I will be expected to move wherever the project may be located. I cannot imagine being responsible for a baby and meeting the demands of my job. Another barrier is the cost of childcare. Infant daycare is more expensive than college tuition, not to mention the cost of diapers and clothes. It is my dream, and I know in my heart I will have a family someday, but it is definitely a daunting prospect to consider.

Single with No Children by Choice

Sabrina is a vibrant, fiercely independent entrepreneur who has built a multi-million-dollar business from the ground up in the construction / oil and gas arena. At fifty, Sabrina has achieved self-defined success and lives a unique, authentic life that involves a healthy balance of growing her business while exploring the world through hiking, skiing, and spending time outdoors.

Sabrina is an only child who is extremely close to her mother and father. She has had serious relationships in the past, but none were ever the right relationship.

> The hardest part of making the decision not to have children was my fear of disappointing my parents. As an only child, I felt the weight of depriving my parents of ever becoming grandparents and felt a tremendous sense of guilt. I believed I was defective in some way because I did not long for a child. By taking the time to really know myself, I knew that my life journey would look different from others. For years, I was uncomfortable when people asked me, "Do you have kids?" My no was met with a look of sympathetic pity, as if my life were a tragedy and could never be complete without reproduction. On the contrary, I live an extremely full life. I have the finances and the freedom to go where I want when I want and have designed an amazing life for myself. My parents often accompany me on adventures, and we travel together frequently. I continue to evolve and change each day and set a new vision each year for myself. I celebrate all aspects of my full life.

Married, No Kids—By Choice

Many women and many couples choose not to have children. In the process, they receive a lot of judgment for it. Bianca has been married to Joe for twenty-five years. They decided early on they did not want to have kids.

> My mother and mother-in-law could not understand. They assumed something was wrong with me and that I could not

conceive. There was nothing further from the truth. Joe and I loved each other, and we were family enough for each other. The ability to have a child and bring it into this world is one that should be taken seriously. It is not for everyone."

Single Mom

Andrea is a single mom to eight-year-old Jake.

I got pregnant in college, and I knew the baby daddy would never be in the picture. I decided to move back to my hometown, where my mother could help me raise Jake while I completed my degree. It took me six years, but I finished, and I immediately got a programming job. I work from home. Jake is in school all day, so my position is ideal. I can still take Jake to school and engage in after-school activities, all while pursuing my career. To make it work, I had to be very clear about what I wanted. I created a list of values and boundaries for my spiritual, professional, personal, and financial lives. It helped me be very focused on the jobs I considered, the men I dated, and how I budget and spend money. Jake was a surprise; I never planned to be a single mom or move back in with my mother. Yet I am making it work. I have a solid career that allows flexibility and a support system; I feel connected to my community, and I have the gift of time to spend with my son. I never would have had any of it if I had not created a plan for my life.

Married Working Mom with Children

Amanda worked as an attorney in a state's attorney's office of appeals.

At eighteen, I had a health issue that resulted in the loss of one fallopian tube. I always knew I wanted a family and children, and the possibility of not being able to conceive haunted me. My husband and I met in high school at fourteen. We stayed together though college and planned to marry when I finished law school. We both knew that the longer I put off starting a family, the higher the odds I would never be a mother. My doctor said if I even could conceive, it might take more than two years, based on my history.

I knew that all of the female attorneys I worked with had intentionally waited to start a family until their midthirties. Female supervisors waited until they were closer to forty and typically had only one child. Most female supervisors did not have children at all. These were the unspoken rules, but I decided I could not abide by them.

We decided to try to start a family, and in less than two months, I was pregnant. At ten weeks, my pregnancy was becoming obvious. One morning, I told my boss about my pregnancy. By that afternoon, I had been transferred out of my position in the city to the suburbs. My boss said it was a coincidence, but I knew the office perception was that a pregnant woman could not handle the pressure of the cases. The irony was that the judge I was assigned to had a reputation for being cruel. My boss may have thought he would be less cruel to a pregnant woman.

A few years later, I was pregnant with my second son. My boss asked me, "Are you planning to take the full six months' maternity leave?" I replied yes. She asked me, "Are you sure? I don't want you to lose your skills with so much time off. You will not be competitive when you return."

I answered, "I don't care. I will be coming back, but I will need the time with my baby."

My boss was not being mean. She was being realistic and wanted me to realize that some people would perceive me as being out of practice. I went on maternity leave, and when I returned, my boss came to see me in my first trial. She commented with surprise, "Wow! You didn't get rusty at all! You did great!"

Like most women in my graduating law class, I decided to make a career change. In my case, I decided to work in the family business. My commitment to my values and my family empowered me to stand in my truth and make decisions that I believed in.

Married Stay-at-Home Mom

Deborah and her husband, James, met in college. Both graduated with a master's in accounting, and both went on to get their CPA licenses.

We got married at twenty-four and had our first son at twenty-six, and I decided to quit my accounting job to stay home. James focused solely on his career and meeting the demands of his job. We were a good team for a long while. As the kids entered high school, I realized that James and I spent absolutely no time together, and I had a pretty lonely existence. We grew more and more distant, and the pressures of raising teenagers, having different parenting styles, and living through years of distance took their toll. We divorced after eighteen years of marriage. I found myself having to start over in my career, which was not an easy feat after fourteen years as a stay-at-home mom. As a CPA during a good economy, the doors opened up quickly, and I got a job right away. Emotionally and professionally, it was daunting. I had to start all over. Everything was different. Technology, work hours, and office expectations put an extraordinary amount of pressure on me to perform. I regretted the decision to stay home. I regretted the divorce for a long time; my life would have been more secure in every way if we had stayed together.

I realized that pining over my past and what could have been was doing nothing for my future. It was holding me back. I started working on myself. It took about three years to readjust to the expectations of work and to find a career that was the right fit for me. Starting over is difficult but sometimes necessary. The important thing was to believe in myself enough to know that I was strong and could make it on my own.

Married, Children, and Career

At thirty years old, I married my husband and moved to Munich, Germany, where he was a captain in the German Air Force. In a few days' time, I went from being a corporate risk manager to a German hausfrau. During the months before the wedding, as I was unraveling my life and preparing to move, every mentor I had asked me, "Are you sure about this? If you leave the country and walk away from your career, you will never get it back." The decision made me nervous, but it did not stop me.

I moved to Germany in August of 1995. I didn't speak a word of German, and I had no prospect of a job, but I was married and drunk on love, excited to finally fulfill my dream of a husband and a family. Unfortunately, I experienced some homesickness and struggled to find my way. I missed my family, friends, and my career. We lived in a one-room apartment in the beautiful city of Munich, which should have been magical, like in my dreams. I was stripped of my support system, culture, language, family, and job identity, all of which took a toll on my marriage.

After five years, lots of battles, and two kids, intertwined with exciting milestones and new experiences, we decided to give my country a try and moved to the United States. When I got back, I was unstoppable. I immediately got a great job, and my attitude, work ethic, and demeanor became different. I stood up straight, I was assertive and confident, and I believed there was nothing I could not do. Living in Germany gave me the courage to stand up for myself and my vision for the life I wanted. My life prepared me for the tough world of construction and, as an executive, of being the only woman in the room. Had I believed the people who told me I would be giving up my career to get married and move away, I would never have gotten where I am today.

Breakthrough

She Knows Herself to Lead Herself

Family can be complicated, and plans are constantly disrupted. It is how we respond to these disruptions that matters. Self-defined success requires one very important principle in life: you must know yourself. To live an authentic life means to spend time getting to know yourself so that you can define your very own mission, vision, and purpose and ultimately set your own value system.

One of my favorite movies is *Under the Tuscan Sun*, the 2003 classic starring Diane Lane. Diane's character, Frances Mayes, is a successful, married San Francisco writer who finds out her husband of twenty years is cheating on her with a twenty-four-year-old who is pregnant. Frances finds herself divorced and alone. Her best friend encourages her to go on a trip to Italy, where Frances finds and purchases a rundown old house in Cortona. Frances always wanted a big family with children, and, through the twists and turns of her life, she ends up with everything she ever wanted, just not in the traditional way she always thought it would happen. Through friendships and relationships, she created her own unique family.

Everyday stories like Frances's occur in real life. But success requires action and a plan. Without them, you are cruising through life, allowing life to happen to you. Knowing yourself requires self-exploration, which takes time and can be uncomfortable.

There is nothing more transformational than someone who takes the time to know herself.

Personally and professionally, I have met people from around the world, and those who know themselves stand out in a crowd. They are energetic and positive, and people naturally gravitate to them. They get things done and are true to their word. They face challenges that could crumble others with tenacity, grace, and commitment. They are committed to lifelong learning. They change and grow as they age. They are rarely stagnant or negative. They know why they are here and live by their personal belief system. Others call them lucky, but luck has less to do with it than intention, energy, attitude, and direction.

People who know themselves lead themselves and see the world in a positive light. They are positive and inspiring. The world needs more of them. Far too many people go through life believing all the lies people tell them or walking aimlessly and angrily to the future. Life is an evolving journey. The stories of the women above are about living an authentic life. Each woman made a decision based on her life circumstances and then went out and lived what life had to offer. Many people told me that if I left my career, started a family, or set an intention to negotiate a flexible schedule, my career would never survive. They were wrong.

Breakthrough Advice for Moms

The following is wise advice that may help you in deciding whether to start a family and how you can move forward:

- The timing is never perfect. There will never be enough money, the perfect job, or the best time.

- Families are not Norman Rockwell paintings. People are emotional and complicated, and starting a family can be stressful. It is normal. It will never be perfect, and it was never meant to be perfect.

- The children will be just fine. My mother used to always tell me that. I worried so much about my job and spending enough time with the children. Each summer, I took them to El Paso to stay for a few weeks with my parents while I provided training across the state for work. They loved everything about that time. Many mothers have asked me how I could be apart from my children for so long. Looking back, it was one of the best things I ever did. My mother died much sooner than ever expected. Now, in their twenties, my kids' best memories of summer include time with their grandma. Those memories would not exist if I had not let them go on their special summer visits.

- Raising kids is expensive, and there is no easy way to do it. Daycare is expensive, in-home care is expensive, and giving up your career to stay home is expensive. What is important is for you to decide for yourself what makes sense for your family. The children will be fine in all of these solutions.

- Love is all they need. Kids need love. Spouses and partners need love. Making baby food, using cloth diapers, and cleaning the house with vinegar to protect the kids from chemicals is all great until those chores create such pressure for the caregiver that she sacrifices her mind and loses sight of the time it takes to show love.

- Don't listen to people who judge you and watch everything you do so that they can tear you down. They are toxic and insecure.

- Your kids are not yours to keep. Your relationships with your children will ebb and flow. There will be good times and bad. Children cannot stay young forever, and you can't stop them from growing up. The more you try to control them, the harder they will push against you. The goal is to create a relationship in which they want to see you, they respect you, and they ask for advice. I dreaded my kids going away to college until my husband told me, "We need to celebrate that they grew up and we did a good job. We did something right. They are out creating their own lives. They know we are here for them, and they will be back because they want to be back."

Set boundaries. Humans need boundaries. We all do, children and adults alike. When you start setting expectations at a young age, kids sense that they are a part of the family unit and have something to contribute. Mothers were not put on this earth to make their kids' lives perfect and hover over them like helicopters. A mother's job is to raise them, guide them, love them, and hold them accountable. We can't prevent failure, but we can be there to pick up the pieces and encourage them to try again when they fall.

Breakthrough Advice: No Children

Women of my generation experienced a lot of judgment when they did not have children. Why would any woman choose to sit out on the amazing, rewarding journey of motherhood? The tide in today's world is now changing. The birthrate in America is the lowest it has been in thirty years.[17] A wide variety of reasons account for the sinking birthrate, including global warming, political unrest, student loans, the cost of daycare, the lack of maternity leave, and the ever-rising cost of health care. These all weigh heavily on a young woman's mind. However, the biggest factor of all is that women finally really have a choice. Society is growing more accepting of people forging their own way in life and making their own decisions. Perhaps our world is finally at a place where the stigma is ending. The decision not to have a child is a personal one. One that must be respected.

Regardless of whether you decide to marry, have a life partner, start a family, or stay single, there is one aspect that impacts the quality of life for all of us: our relationship with money. The following chapter addresses women's long and complicated relationship with money and the importance of developing healthy financial habits in order to achieve self-defined success.

Chapter 6
Budgets

Budget:

1. A statement of the financial position of an administration (as of a nation) for a definite period of time based on estimates of expenditures during the period and proposals for financing them.
2. A plan for the coordination of resources and expenditures.
3. The amount of money that is available for, required for, or assigned to a particular purpose.

Money. It is one of the most convoluted, challenging, and difficult issues facing women of all ages. Money is its own foreign language. It requires study, dedication, and time to master it. Yet it is one of the most important things for women to use wisely in order to achieve self- defined success.

Most Americans have a combination of sources of debt, including credit cards, student loans, mortgages, car loans, and personal loans. And despite their best intentions, Americans are digging themselves deeper into the hole each year. The average American now has about $38,000 in personal debt, excluding home mortgages.[18] The following issues compound money problems.

Women . . .

- make less money. There has been slow progress, but women are still paid 80 percent on the dollar compared to men. Less money means less opportunity to accrue retirement savings.[19]
- work fewer years. Due to the responsibilities of caring for children and aging parents, women work more part-time jobs than men. Often, women work in jobs that are considered to be hobbies. Fewer hours worked and lower wages means fewer payments into the Social Security system. That means that when a woman retires, she may not receive her full retirement benefit.[20]
- live longer than men. It is genetically proven that women can live, on average, six to eight years longer than men.[21] That means women need more retirement funds.
- have more student debt. Today, two-thirds of the more than $1.3 trillion in total US loan debt are owed by women. With lower earnings, it takes women longer to pay back such debt and reduces their ability to save for retirement.[22]

All women, regardless of their marital status—single, divorced, widowed, or married—must own and actively manage their financial lives. A lack of confidence about personal finance decisions has long been a source of frustration for women, hindering their ability to take greater control of family finances and, ultimately, their retirement.

Beware the Illusion of Security

What about a woman in a stable relationship with a partner who takes care of everything? Why would she need to understand money? The answer is simple: so that in the event that the breadwinner dies, cheats, becomes disabled, or disappears, she will not be financially devastated. In the event of a divorce, alimony may not be available. In the past, the stay-at-home spouse received cost-of-living payments from their ex. That is not necessarily the case anymore. There is a universal trend of putting more limits on the length of support and more standardization on the sums doled out. The laws vary by state, and in many cases, maintenance is denied altogether, even for women who have not worked for decades.

Joanna's Story

Joanna was married to Steve, an attorney. They met in college, and she worked as an insurance account manager while he went to law school. Upon graduating, Steve was on the fast track to partner and was earning $250,000 a year. They decided to start a family, so Joanna stayed home. The day their youngest son left for college, her husband packed a bag and moved out. He was in love with his assistant, who was the same age as their oldest son. Since Joanna and Steve lived in Texas, they found that state law did not require alimony payments. Joanna was not eligible for child support payments because both of their boys were over eighteen. She hired a lawyer—one that she could not really afford; her husband's was the best divorce lawyer in town. During the final hearing, the judge actually admonished Joanna for staying home for so long, saying, "You had a degree and skills . . . It's about time you go back to work!" Joanna had not worked in decades. She could not use a computer. So she took classes at the local community college and finally found a job as a receptionist at a school. She could not make ends meet each month. She could not help her sons with their education. Her ex moved on and started another family. He decided he couldn't afford to help the boys with college.

María's Story

María was a stay-at-home mom with two ten-year-old twin girls. When she was thirty-nine years of age, her husband—José, age forty-two and the love of her life—was a successful CFO for a large privately held company. They had a great life—a beautiful home, private schools, a boat, and a small lake house. They traveled every summer on different destination vacations. One day, José suffered a massive stroke that left him paralyzed on one side and impacted his short-term memory. He needed twenty-four-hour full-time health care and was no longer able to work. He had life insurance and long-term disability. The life insurance was useless because he was still alive. The long-term disability paid 60 percent of his previous salary. It did not include bonuses. After eighteen months, the family needed to pay Cobra to keep the health insurance from his employer, which was more than $1,800 a month for a family of four, not including the deductibles and copayments. María set up a GoFundMe page to which all her friends and family contributed, raising $10,000. This was a drop in the bucket compared to the bills that were coming in. His treatment required round-the-clock care for the rest of his life. The house had a full mortgage, and they had very little savings. The cars had been bought on lease. Ultimately, they lost their home, the girls changed to public schools, and they ended up moving in with José's parents to help with his care and all the bills.

Prior to the stroke, María and José had spoken often about savings and insurance. He'd always said he had it under control. She never looked at the bank accounts; she didn't even know the passwords; they had no will, medical directive, or power of attorney. Since they were young, they thought they didn't need to worry about all those things. In the first few weeks after the stroke, José could not communicate, and María did not even know how to log in to their bank account. When she finally did, she realized they had lived paycheck to paycheck for the last ten years and had no savings, no equity in their home or their lake house, and no emergency fund.

Both Joanna and María had chosen to depart the workplace. That was not their problem. Deciding to leave was part of their own personal definition of self-defined success. Their problems stemmed from assuming that the breadwinner would successfully take care of all the family's financial needs and plan for the future. Such laxity can result in financial disaster and unnecessary heartache.

Single and Delayed Saving

Married women are not the only ones who delay financial planning. Single women tend to make the same mistake. Deborah, a thirty-four-year-old doctor, lives in Chicago in an expensive high-rise apartment that is close to the hospital where she works. She is finally making money for the first time in years. She has more than $100,000 in student loan debt and takes pride in paying her bills on time while living on a budget. She was offered a 401(k), but she turned it down. Deborah did not think she could pay her rent and student loans and also save for retirement. She has trouble making ends meet each month. She figures she will start saving when she is older. Unfortunately, she thinks, *I have plenty of time to worry about retirement. Why start now?* Many single women recognize that financial planning is a necessity, but they have bought into the limiting belief that they can't afford to save. The reality is they can't afford not to.

Limiting Beliefs about Money

So many limiting beliefs around money permeate women's brains. My own personal favorites include:

- Money is the root of all evil.
- Money changes everything.

- Money doesn't grow on trees.
- A certain amount of money would change my life.
- If I only had more money, I would be happy.
- Everyone is in debt, so why not me?

Breakthrough: Personal

Here are some things women can do to shake away old limiting beliefs about money and replace them with solid strategies that lead to making sound financial decisions.

1. **Make a Budget:** Start simple by listing what money is coming into the household and what is going out. What are your monthly expenses, such as food, utilities, and rent? Stop going out to eat and splurging on coffee. It is not worth it. Even if you are barely making ends meet, look for ways to cut back. You may save a little bit of money on memberships or extravagances that you don't really need.

2. **Prioritize:** If you are paying a monthly fee for a gym or class and haven't used it, cancel the membership. The fee can be used for something else or to pay off a bill. Look into cheaper alternatives for other expenses. Identify where you may be splurging yet thinking it's a bargain. Sales and Groupons are great, but you still have to pay for them in the end.

3. **Respect Your Credit:** Never take out a credit card to get a 10 percent discount at a store. Use one credit card for everything, and pay it off at the end of the month. If you can't afford that sweater today, you won't be able to afford it next month at 25 percent interest either. Be leery of overextending your credit. When purchasing a car, opt for what you actually can afford;

think about the long-term commitment, not only what you can afford in a monthly payment. Consider shopping for certified, leased preowned vehicles that are about two years old. The apartment with the spectacular view won't be that great if you can't afford your rent or become house poor. Stop coveting what others have, and watch your bank account grow. There is no better feeling in life than going to sleep knowing that your bills are paid and that you have some cash in the bank.

4. **Invest in Retirement:** First, check with your employer to see if you can enroll in your company's 401(k) plan. You can also set up an individual retirement account. The US Treasury website outlines a two-step process for transferring your account balance to a Roth IRA and offers tips on what to consider when selecting a provider.

5. **Protect against the Unknown:** Look into health insurance and other types of coverage to hedge against risk. Never go without health insurance. Buy renter's insurance and, if you own a home, flood insurance.

6. **Get a Financial Education:** Seek out a reputable financial advisor, or talk to a trusted friend about tips for saving for retirement or other questions you may have. Take a free class on the internet.

7. **Know Where You Are and Where You Want to Go:** Whether you are married or not, you must have an understanding of your financial situation. Know the accounts and passwords. Ask questions about savings, and review financial statements. Log in to retirement accounts regularly, and balance the checkbook. By staying active and involved in your financial situation, you can plan and recognize warning signs and ward off painful financial decisions that can lead to ruin.

Money and Business

The concepts of finance and accounting are applied throughout every industry in the world. Whether you are starting a small business or growing a large organization, an understanding of finances and some basic accounting knowledge set the foundation for success.

Too many women aim to move up the corporate ladder or get a promotion only to be stymied because they can't speak the language of money by conveying a basic understanding of finance and accounting. Personally, for the first ten years of my career, I absolutely hated accounting and worked hard to stay away from it. Later, I realized that to accurately and loudly state a business case that was in need of support from the CFO and executive team, I needed to understand the impact to the bottom line.

My Money Story

In my past role as a safety professional, my team wanted to implement a wellness program for our field workers. I was passionately excited about the idea. I knew this would bring much-needed medical screening for diabetes and heart disease as well as healthy best practices to an overlooked community. Full of excitement, I went to meet with the CFO to discuss the idea. He quickly shot it down. My pitch focused only on the outcome of changing the world for people. I did not discuss or bring up the budget. A few months passed as my team worked on budgets, time commitments, schedules, and venues. I pitched my proposal again, this time including a budget and a forecast of money saved on claims due to a healthier workplace. My program was approved. In my first pitch, I was speaking from my heart. In my second, the CFO and I were speaking the same language.

With any project, there needs to be a sound financial reason to support investing in it or to warrant a catalyst for change. There also need to be financial reports that include budgets and projections to support it.

Don't Limit Yourself through Self-Deprecating Comments

In spite of studying business in college, I barely survived the accounting classes, which grew into my own limiting belief around my ability to understand accounting and finance. I often joked at work, "I am not an accountant!" As a result, when it came to certain aspects of my job related to budgets or purchasing insurance, I realized that I had undermined my own credibility and hindered my ability to get to the next level. My perceived inability to understand basic accounting principles and read a standard balance sheet hurt my reputation. My self-deprecating attitude around finance actually gave my colleagues permission to dismiss me. When it came down to deciding who was right for an upcoming project, I provided the executive team the excuse they needed to disqualify me. It became common knowledge that "Tricia would be great, but she doesn't understand the financial implications." All of my credentials and experience didn't matter. I was perceived as the woman who couldn't understand basic financial accounting principles. When I finally stopped joking about my limitations and got serious about understanding top-line and bottom-line performance, my credibility and my career soared.

Breakthrough: Business

Every woman, of every age and every profession, whether she is married, unmarried, employed, a stay-at-home mom, a part-time entrepreneur, an artist, a writer, or in possession of another creative talent, must have a basic understanding of finances, for both personal and professional reasons. Take a course online, read a book or the *Wall Street Journal,* find a mentor, or ask an accountant. Take action to make sure you are relatively well versed in the language of finance and accounting. Here is a list of online resources to get your started.

- **SuzeOrman.com:** Suze Orman is a money expert and a self-made millionaire who has dedicated her life to helping women become more knowledgeable about money.

- **JeanChatzky.com:** Jean Chatzky has a superpower. She takes the complicated world of money and explains it so people can actually understand it. Her website is full of tools and information to help you.

- **SBA.gov:** The Small Business Administration offers classes and free resources for any entrepreneur wanting to start or grow a business.

In addition, your local colleges will provide continuing education classes both online and in person for a relatively inexpensive price. If your employer offers a 401(k) program and you are enrolled, they may provide free resources on investment strategies. Check your employment handbook to see whether your employer has an education reimbursement benefit. You may be able to take finance-related classes and get reimbursed.

Commit to looking into one resource before you finish reading this book. If you are a married woman who relies solely on your spouse to handle the money, I implore you to schedule time to sit down and review the finances. If your spouse is hesitant to share statements, accounts, and passwords with you, it may be a red flag for financial trouble in the future.

Did you know that the fear of bankruptcy is one of women's biggest fears in life? Based on the stories we have just read, it is no wonder that issues related to money are among women's primary fears. We will explore that fear and some of its causes in the next chapter.

Chapter 7
Bankruptcy

> *Being broke is temporary. Being poor is a state of mind.*
>
> —Unknown

Bankrupt:

1. A debtor (such as an individual or an organization) whose property is subject to voluntary or involuntary administration under the bankruptcy laws for the benefit of the debtor's creditors.
2. A person who becomes insolvent.

The previous chapter discussed the importance of saving and why women need to develop a healthy relationship with money in both their personal and professional lives. I was surprised how often the word "bankrupt" came up during the interviews for this book. Women commented that their worst fear, from a financial perspective, was becoming bankrupt. Several women also referred to being emotionally bankrupt when things didn't go as expected or they were feeling exhausted and alone.

This chapter explores bankruptcy in terms of two limiting beliefs that impact women both personally and professionally: poverty consciousness and the prosperity illusion.

Poverty Consciousness

Arielle Ford, a celebrated love and relationship expert, author, and speaker, coined the term *poverty consciousness* when she realized that her beliefs about a lack of money were impacting her marriage:

> I didn't know I was living in a poverty consciousness mindset until I got married. My husband grew up in a very affluent home where his mother raised him to buy only the best of everything. By contrast, I grew up in a home where every single day meant World War III over money. Most of my clothes were hand-me-downs from other people. I never bought anything new that wasn't discounted. *There was never enough.* And suddenly I met this guy who was buying $75 bottles of wine.
>
> One time, we were on a book tour in Cleveland, and it started to snow. He needed to buy a coat, and it was $600 dollars. I was shocked, and I said, "$600!" I have never paid more than $75 for a coat. He looked at me like I was crazy and said, "The last coat I bought was a $2,000 Armani, and I have had it for fifteen years." I thought *Oh my God, why am I so triggered by this?* As I started thinking about it, I realized I had all this fear around becoming a bag lady—homeless and not having enough money.
>
> I had never shared any of this with my husband. But I did finally sit my husband down one night and said, "We had totally different childhoods. Money was always an issue in my family. That is why I worked so hard and have saved everything I ever made. I realize that for you it was different. I don't want to police you around money, but we have to figure this out. "
>
> We came up with a creative solution. We decided to have three bank accounts: My Money, Your Money, and Our

Money. In the Our Money account, we agreed that no one would spend more than $500 without having a conversation about it. I no longer had to have the money concern, and my husband didn't have to look over his shoulder every time he made a purchase.

Statistically, the number-one cause for divorce is money. In most couples, one is a spender, and one is a saver. We assume that one is bad or wrong, which creates tension that leads to arguments and stress. Just because someone has a different philosophy doesn't mean that they are wrong or that they are bad.

Creative solutions require a couple to have grown-up conversations in which each party speaks their truth without someone being judged as wrong. It requires timing and thought. The conversation can't take place when you are mad. Rather than coming from an angry place, the conversation must begin from a responsible place.

To start a creative solution conversation, ask your partner to set a convenient time to talk for ten minutes. You don't need longer than that. Start the conversation by saying, "I have a problem." Then clearly state the problem. "I have a fear about spending money. I have always saved my money, and my fear is that I won't have enough, and I could end up a bag lady."

The next step is to explore ways to make it better. As a result of our creative solution, I have learned to appreciate quality, having nice things, and that paying retail sometimes is OK. And my husband has learned to shop sales.

Prosperity Illusion

On the other side of the spectrum from poverty consciousness is the damaging notion of prosperity illusion. Since the late 1800s,

women have moved in and out of the economy based on demand for work, and from the beginning, they have performed the brunt of the mostly unpaid work of household duties such as childcare, overall caregiving, and housekeeping.[23]

In the late 1800s, women became the natural target for a relatively new kind of sales force called direct sales marketing. Traditionally, a common career path for men was door-to-door sales. These salesmen had bad reputations for being swindlers because they came into towns and sold products that didn't perform as they should, leaving the buyer with no recourse while the salesmen were never seen again. To combat this scheme, the government began to implement regulations. However, these men realized that by empowering women—often marginalized citizens of society—these women could sell more products in homes, avoiding regulations and being paid less than door-to-door salesmen. Thus, they created elaborate schemes to bypass the regulations, which included direct sales marketing and in-home parties. Today, this type of organization is called a pyramid scheme, and it often verges on being illegal.

In the 1800s, however, these opportunities were attractive to stay-at-home moms, who were responsible for the duties of the home and as such were not able to leave to work in the outside world. So why not find a way for women to sell from their homes? This method provided connection, social support, and an opportunity for women to get together and socialize while selling products and recruiting others to sell as well. There was an expectation that women would be paid less than men. It was understood. Furthermore, women were already used to participating in an informal economy by selling baked goods or making clothes to help make ends meet. In spite of the opportunity to earn money and independence, the fact is that these women were victims of unfair labor practices that benefitted men.

These direct sales schemes flourished because it was understood that women could accommodate care of their children and

husbands while supporting the notion of domesticity. The reality is that while thousands of women joined such companies, very little income was actually made. However, women were rewarded socially, and, for the first time, they received not only a paycheck but also much-needed affirmation and appreciation, which built self-confidence and esteem. Even if the checks were not as lucrative as promised, the social experience was intoxicating and brought joy, connection, and positivity to a mundane and often isolated life. In other words, women who signed up for these schemes were trapped as underlings to men in a system that took advantage of them.

Direct sales schemes were the foundation of an industry known as *multilevel marking*, which now employs billions of people around the world. The key to growing a business is recruiting others to become part of your own sales force. One of the strategies for recruitment—and the ultimate success of the sales force—is based on "chasing prosperity." It is a belief that, first and foremost, we all deserve things. Next, to be successful in recruiting others, key components include positivity, being yourself, affirmations, and a common-sense approach stating that if you work hard and are a good person, good things will come to you. The upside of the prosperity chase is that, for many people, it is the first time they have been exposed to techniques that build assertiveness, confidence, and a can-do attitude.

The downside to this practice is that those who can't afford the investment in products or who fail at recruiting others to join end up being blamed for the failure—and, worse, end up blaming themselves. Their failure is not presented by these organizations as the result of a saturated market or waning demand for products. These disadvantages are presented as personal failures. The idea is that if, for some reason, someone doesn't succeed in the selling and recruiting process, it is 100 percent entirely that individual's fault.

When failure strikes, it can be another blow to the ego, as the failed salesperson believes that they are the only one who couldn't succeed, that it is their fault, and that they are flawed in some way. Remember the definition of bliss: a calm state of mind that is achieved when your thoughts, actions, and words are in alignment. One of the most common symptoms of misalignment is debt. You will never experience bliss if you can't pay your bills.

I do believe that many of our challenges in life are based in the baggage we bring with us from our past and our upbringing, as well as in our outdated and obsolete views of money. However, believing that we will become prosperous is not enough. Jumping into the first thing that comes along and investing money you don't have can actually contribute to financial ruin.

As the barriers to entry keeping women from higher-paying jobs that lead to more lucrative career paths are torn down, perhaps the draw of multilevel marketing schemes will diminish.

Both poverty consciousness and false prosperity are extremes. The challenge is to recognize and change limiting beliefs around money while simultaneously setting realistic expectations. The right dose of scrutiny, a positive belief system, and a strong work ethic are needed to achieve your vision of self-defined success in a fashion and on a timeline that are realistic and strategic. It is important not to fall prey to the extremes or to unfair labor practices; be wary and cautious, and evaluate all aspects of an opportunity before taking the leap.

Breakthrough

What Is True Prosperity?

I have identified two extremes stemming from false beliefs around prosperity. Women on the path to developing their own authentic life based on self-defined success must get their vision of true prosperity clear. The following are the four qualities of true prosperity.

The Four Bs of True Prosperity

1. **Bliss:** A calm state of mind that is achieved when your thoughts, actions, and words are in alignment.

2. **Bravery:** The courage to make choices to achieve bliss. Those choices may impact important people in your life who do not agree or act in your best interest. Alignment in your thoughts, actions, and words may require you to change toxic or unhealthy patterns in your life. It may require you to say no for the first time. And the more you stand in your truth, the braver you will become.

3. **Blessings:** When you share your talents, love, attention, and gifts with others, you are passing on a blessing and receiving one in turn. Generosity is the offering of a blessing given freely and out of pure love. No strings attached. No expectations.

4. **Bounce:** A sense of happiness that, like bubbles in a glass of champagne, rises to the top of the glass. The more you achieve bliss, exercise bravery, and share blessings, the more abundant your bounce and the more happy moments you will experience in your life. When we are bouncing up, we are happy and in the best possible place to be good to ourselves and those we love.

There is always one—often more than one—quality that is broken or not present at all. Identifying the missing qualities and talking through ways to bring all of them to the forefront is a key step in identifying issues that hold you back. Does it immediately solve a financial problem? Of course not. But it becomes the foundation that propels women from feeling overwhelmed or defeated to feeling empowered and in control of their futures. It's the catalyst to self-defined success.

> **Since when do you let others make decisions for you? You've earned the right to be here.**
>
> —Pat Connorton (my mother)

Chapter 8
Bias

> *The eyes see only what the eyes are prepared to comprehend.*
>
> —Robertson Davies

Bias:
1. An inclination of temperament or outlook, especially a personal and sometimes unreasoned judgment.
2. Prejudice.

Unconscious bias is tricky because people are unaware of the biases they hold. This chapter addresses some of the peculiar and unique external challenges women face as they progress in their career or return to a career after a period of time off.

Unconscious bias describes discrimination and incorrect judgments that occur due to stereotyping. These can occur automatically and without the person being aware of them. These types of biases are often so ingrained in a culture and society that they go unnoticed by many people.

A Harvard business study was launched to reveal how different words used in performance reviews impacted decisions in the workplace.[24] The researchers focused on the military, the most traditional, longstanding, male-dominated work environment. Over the last several decades, the military has also worked diligently to eliminate formal gender segregation and discrimination. The military's performance evaluation tools are predicated on meritocratic ideals of fairness and justice, intentionally designed to provide equal opportunity regardless of a person's demographics. The analysis spanned more than four thousand participants and eighty-one thousand evaluations that included a list of eighty-nine positive and negative leadership attributes used to assess leadership performance in a military setting. The results showed no difference between genders in objective measures such as grades, fitness scores, or class standing. There was also no difference in the number of positive attributes assigned. However, the positive words used to describe men and women were very different. Positive words to describe men included analytical, competent, athletic, and dependable. Positive words for women included compassionate, enthusiastic, energetic, and organized.

Women were assigned significantly more negative attributes. The most common negative attribute used to describe men was arrogant, followed by irresponsible. Women were described as inept, frivolous, gossipy, excitable, scattered, temperamental, panicky, and indecisive. The research showed that the attributes we use to describe male and female leaders are more than just words, and they can have real-life implications.

So, what is the big deal about the difference in word choice? If two equal candidates are being evaluated for a leadership role and one is described as compassionate while the other is described as analytical, who will get the promotion? Unless the field is nursing or education, an analytical person may have an advantage. Conversely, consider a manager determining the dismissal of two equal candidates. One is described as arrogant, while the other is inept. Which will be the first to be let go?

Subtle Bias versus Blatant Bias

Social science data shows that people are much more likely to encounter subtle forms of bias than overt ones. Today, HR professionals may rarely hear female subordinates complain of blatant overtures such as catcalls. Instead, managers may choose to subtly ignore a woman's input. These behaviors may be unintentional and can reflect unconscious beliefs about the characteristics of women. Some might argue that the general evolution of discrimination from obvious to subtle may be evidence of social progress. Unfortunately, research shows that the new kind of bias can be even worse than the older kind.[25]

Unconscious Bias Collides with High Performance

Lauren was a project manager for an oil and gas company in Texas. For the first two years in her role, she was considered a high performer and was consistently offered high-profile projects that spanned departments. She had a reputation as the go-to person to get complex projects completed on time and on budget. Lauren was told by her boss, the project executive, that she had been brought in to be a change agent and to finally break down the long-standing silos that existed between various departments. During her annual performance review, her boss assigned two goals: "mentor other women by starting a women's leadership group and continue to work on multidepartmental projects in order to ultimately break down preexisting silos." Being the professional go-getter that she was, Lauren got to work. She set up a series of women's leadership meetings. They were a hit, with staff attending monthly. Lauren appointed leaders, and the team created a mission, vision, and strategic plan for the group. The plan included hosting a book study on Sheryl Sandburg's latest book, *Option B: Facing Adversity, Building Resilience, and Finding Joy*. More than 70 percent of the office staff joined the book group.

During this time, Lauren was assigned big multidepartment projects for which she was creating crossdepartmental teams. The study group actually allowed her to engage with people she never would have met before. This translated into alignment on project team engagement because she was able to develop more personal relationships with people from other departments. Lauren was on fire. She felt invigorated and unstoppable. Until . . .

A young female from administration who attended the study approached her boss. She asked, "Can I set up a time to discuss my future with you?" Her boss awkwardly and noncommittally skulked away, wondering, *Where is she coming from? She's an admin! What future?* Another woman asked her boss, "Are there any plans to adopt or implement a more flexible schedule?" to which he replied, "Ah! No. We would lose control if that ever happened."

Unbeknownst to Lauren, these incidents and Lauren became the talk of the boardroom. For the first time ever, the board had to begrudgingly discuss how to handle these ambitious administrative women. One executive actually commented, "What is getting into these people? They are really ruining it for everyone." The executives didn't appreciate the staff expecting a career path and having the nerve to ask questions. The board members secretly discussed their frustration. "Thanks to Lauren's little Women's Powwow, the turnover is going to skyrocket out of control. Can't people be happy with a steady paycheck?"

In hindsight, Lauren surmised, "I should have seen all the signs that I was making the executive team uncomfortable." Instead, she just kept doing what she thought she was supposed to do.

Then Lauren noticed changes in the way her boss was treating her. She was no longer invited to lunch with the other project managers, and direction on assignments was limited. Her boss seemed exasperated when Lauren asked a question. She noticed some sarcasm but chalked it up to her boss being stressed and overworked. When it came time for Lauren's next performance review, she was blindsided. "It was the worst I have ever had in my career. In spite of working harder than I ever had before, I was given a below-average performance ranking, which meant I did not receive a bonus or a raise. My boss's comments used vague words like, 'You tend to be scattered in meetings. You spend too much time on pet projects,' referring to the women's leadership initiative he asked me to create." Lauren initially attempted to fight back and provide her own side of the story. Her boss became agitated and condescending. "He was not interested in any of it, and I could tell by the look on his face that he was getting a sick satisfaction out of putting me in my place."

This was the beginning of the end. The relationship deteriorated as the job requirements morphed and evolved at the whim of Lauren's boss. He began to micromanage her time, second guess her work, and regard her with visible disdain. Lauren started looking for another job and got out as soon as she could. The women's leadership group disbanded. She was no longer on the high-profile career track. "My career definitely took a hit. I had to leave before my self-confidence was completely shattered."

Physically Pushed Out by Bias

Unconscious bias can take physical form as well. Courtney worked as a quality director at a large jobsite in Oregon. She is a professional engineer with years of construction experience, and she is most often the only woman on a project. During a project team meeting, the group of male colleagues was discussing solving a quality issue on the project.

> There were four of us standing in a project trailer in a circle. We were brainstorming solutions to fix the quality issue. As I, as the quality director for the project, was about to give my assessment of the situation, I noticed the project manager next to me slowly moving closer and closer. The circle was actually getting smaller. While I was still stating my solution, he began to physically nudge

me out so that I suddenly found myself standing outside the circle. I was angry and frustrated. The other men all stepped closer together, and I was physically pushed out. I felt like my years of experience and suggestions to fix the problem were being ignored. As I took a seat at the table and began working on my reports, I heard the project manager who had nudged me out of the circle suggest the exact same solution that I had just recommended. Word for word. My idea became his idea, and they implemented the fix.

The Challenge of Obscurity and Bias

The challenge with bias is that, according to scientific study, what happens automatically is by definition outside of our control, triggered by our brain making quick judgments and assessments of people and situations, which are influenced by our background, cultural environment, and personal experiences.[26]

Proponents of training to fix this problem may be missing the mark. Some experts argue that training people to understand their own biases is a waste of time. Training assumes that once someone is aware of their own bias, that awareness will help them correct their thinking and that they will change their behavior and censor their own thoughts. This assumes that by merely exposing a bias, it will ultimately and magically evaporate. Furthermore, it wrongly assumes that when someone is aware of a bias, they will actually want to change it. Exposure may help a person gain insight, but insight does not mean someone wants to change their behavior. Unfortunately, people may choose to hover under the umbrella of unconscious bias as a way of legitimizing their prejudices.[27]

Research has also provided evidence that in some cases, training about unconscious biases has increased defensiveness, reinforced stereotypes, and contributed to stonewalling, which ultimately are all expressions of anger, frustration, and resentment. Underlying these emotions is fear—fear of losing power, of losing status, of losing rewards, of our credibility being undermined, of our own ignorance, and of how people with different opinions will change the ways things are done in the workplace.[28]

Further research shows that groups in an organization that are dominant in terms of gender, race, nationality, or ways of working are all motivated to maintain the status quo. Dominance amounts to power.[29] Why would you want to give your power away or even share some of it?

Fear and power are at the heart of keeping things the same. To address fear and power, we need to plough into the root of these emotions. Once we know where the emotions stem from, then we can begin to plant the seeds for new behaviors. Other organizational concepts—such as fitting in to the office culture, which also corresponds to the view that we like people who are like us—are equally contentious and make up a part of the equation that is organizational culture.

Breakthrough

According to the Office of Diversity and Outreach of the University of California, San Francisco, to identify and ultimately change unconscious biases, they must be addressed personally by individuals and professionally by the leaders of organizations.[30]

Personally, unconscious bias can hold you back from becoming your authentic self by stifling growth and letting you hang on to falsehoods and limiting beliefs (chapter 2, "Beliefs").

Professionally, unconscious bias stifles creativity by constructing an echo chamber within an organization in which change will never occur. The reality is that the world is changing and dynamic, and businesses must embrace the change to be successful for the long-term years to come.

Personal Strategies

Unconscious biases are difficult to change . . . but not impossible. Research suggests that there are actions we can take and techniques we can utilize to minimize the impact of unconscious bias on our thoughts and behaviors.[31]

The following strategies can be used to address unconscious bias at the individual level.

- **Education:** By reading this chapter and learning about unconscious bias, you have taken the first step to addressing some of your biases. Consider taking the next step by participating in an unconscious bias training program to learn more about the origins and consequences of biases and strategies to address prejudices.

- **Self-Awareness:** In addition to education, enhanced self-awareness is a powerful tool in addressing unconscious bias. Recognizing biases toward a particular group is yet another step you can take to minimizing the impact of prejudice on your actions and behaviors.

- **Project Implicit:**[32] This nonprofit organization and international collaboration between researchers is interested in implicit social cognition—thoughts and feelings outside of conscious awareness and control. The goal of the organization is to educate the public about hidden biases. The online Implicit Association Test (IAT) is a valuable tool individuals can use to learn more about their biases. You can take various self-assessments at Implicit.Harvard.edu/implicit/takeatest.html.

- **Explore and Engage:** Intentionally seek out and engage in discussions with colleagues from diverse groups, or volunteer in a community that's socially dissimilar to your own. This can lead to greater appreciation and perhaps minimize the impact of unconscious bias on others.

Unconscious Bias in Business

Organizations must also commit to taking steps to mitigate the impact of unconscious bias.

- **Hiring and Promotion Practices:** Develop ground rules to ensure equity in the hiring and promotion process. For example, search committees should develop and utilize concrete, objective indicators and outcomes to reduce relying on standard stereotypes. This includes structured interviews and objective evaluation criteria. Search committees should allocate sufficient time to review and discuss candidates in a structured manner, as unconscious bias may be more pervasive when under time pressure or when making quick decisions.

- **Awareness:** Organizations should open a conversation about unconscious bias to create awareness and strive to identify issues that permeate their industry.

- **Leadership:** Organizations should provide leaders with support and guidance to address unconscious bias but also require that efforts and outcomes be documented through an annual summary.

While bias may be unconscious, it can inadvertently lead to bullying on the playground and at work. Children, after all, pick up their first set of beliefs at home. In the next chapter, I will explore how bullying is a behavior that starts early in childhood and occurs often. Bullies are alive and well in business settings and can derail a woman's career.

Chapter 9
Bullies

Bully:

1. A blustering, browbeating person, especially one who is habitually cruel, insulting, or threatening to others who are weaker, smaller, or in some way vulnerable.

The eighth B word is bullies. As we go through life, we think of a bully as a menace on the playground who steals lunch money. Yet that is just the beginning. Bullying starts early, happens often, and can plague the workplace.

Bullying is such an epic problem in the United States school system that the government has actually created an antibullying website (StopBullying.gov) and the month of October has been designated National Bullying Prevention Month.

- One in four US students says they have been bullied at school.
- Bullying affects all youth, including those who are bullied, those who bully others, and those who see bullying going on. Some effects may last into adulthood.

- Bullying is usually not a simple interaction between a student who bullies and a student who is bullied. Instead, it often involves groups of students who support each other in bullying other students.

Two modes of bullying are direct and indirect. Direct means the bullying is out in the open, visibly directed at the target—such as name calling and physical assault. Indirect is when the bully spreads rumor and innuendo behind the target's back. In addition to these modes, the four types of bullying include the broad categories of physical, verbal, relational, (harming the reputation or relationships of the targeted youth), and damage to property.

The Target

Children who are bullied—referred to as "targets"—are perceived as different from their peers in some way, perhaps by being overweight or underweight, wearing glasses or different clothing, being new to a school, or being unable to afford what kids consider "cool." They are perceived as weak or unable to defend themselves and may be depressed or anxious or have low self-esteem. These victims are regarded by other children as less popular, which contributes to their inability to make connections and friends. They are regarded as annoying, provocative, or attention seeking; they ultimately get labeled as people who don't get along with others.

The Bully

There are two kinds of bullies. The first kind is well connected to their peers, has social power, is overly concerned about their popularity, and likes to dominate or be in charge of others. The second kind is isolated from their peers and may be depressed or anxious, have low self-esteem, be less involved in school, be easily pressured by peers, or not identify with the emotions or feelings of others.

The CDC states that the key to bullying prevention is adults responding quickly and consistently to bullying behavior and sending a message that it is not acceptable. Key players in bullying prevention include parents, school staff, and adults in the community who can intervene, provide guidance, and create a bullying prevention program.

The Impact of Bullies on Girls and Women

Bullying begins as early as four years old in kindergarten and pre-K and crescendos into full-blown attacks in middle school. If you were anything like me in middle school, it was not an easy journey. I had frizzy red hair, braces, and octagonal, wire-rimmed Coke-bottle glasses. I was indeed "under construction." I was the only person in my school with freckles. I wore a sweat jacket all summer to cover the freckles on my arms in middle school even though it was one hundred degrees in Texas. With her red hair, quirky style, and freckles, Molly Ringwald in the movie *Sixteen Candles* was my idol. She gave girls like me hope!

The following portraits of different types of girls show the journeys many face as they navigate the road to womanhood. See if any of these journeys resonates with you.

Awkward Girl

As girls grow into women, many go through a difficult phase during which growing pains like acne, growth spurts, and braces are visible to the world. Awkward Girl realizes in middle school that friends from childhood aren't friends anymore. School changes from a playground to a warzone. Her best friend from elementary school morphs into the queen of sixth grade and even has a "court" of three other girls who worship her and follow her around. They dress alike by wearing their hair up in high half ponytails with scrunchies that match their iridescent T-shirts. Awkward Girl always gets to class early to secure a seat in the back of the room in hopes that she will fade away into her little desk. Queeny and her court saunter into class. Queeny wears her popularity like a tiara. Awkward Girl's whole body uncontrollably winces as they float into the classroom. Queeny calls out to Awkward Girl in a syrupy tone, "You look so pretty today!" as her court snickers and laughs. The teacher intervenes, commanding, "Stop it! Be quiet!" Queeny responds, "Why? I paid her a compliment!" This produces louder laughter. Awkward Girl wonders, *What did I ever do to her to deserve this? Why is she so mean? When will this ever stop?*

Invisible Girl

Time passes, and Awkward Girl starts high school. After three years of practice in middle school, becoming Invisible Girl is easy. She is never included in social events; she withdraws and spends her weekends at home. She is labeled socially awkward. Her parents encourage her: "Why don't you get out more? Join a group? Go to a dance. Remember that high school is the best time of your life."

Only Woman

Invisible Girl survives high school. College is a welcome respite from the torture of high school; she pursues a degree in construction management. Upon graduation, she lands a job as a project engineer on a construction site. She finds herself the Only Woman on a project. The first couple of days, she notices the "locker-room talk." The guys talk loudly and proudly to each other. "Hey, I got some last night." Noticing Only Woman, one of them chides, "Hey, do you need a date this weekend? I can write your number inside the Porta Potti wall and see who takes the bait!"

At first, Only Woman accepts this behavior as a normal part of construction. She thinks to herself, *I just need to toughen up.* As time goes on, things escalate. Her boss, Rob, the project superintendent, is in his forties, a burly man who liked his beer and has the stomach to show for it. His ego and attitude are as big as his gut. He flirts, which progresses to bear hugs, pats on the head, and unrequited advances that result in humiliation and control tactics.

Rob abruptly changes Only Woman's work hours so she can no longer pick up her kids from school. One Monday, Rob summons Only Woman to the trailer conference room, where a group of men are sitting around the makeshift conference table. Rob says, "Take a seat over there next to the coffee pot." He then leers at her, saying, "That's right; just like that." She winces and replies, "Rob, what do you need?" He sneers, "Nothing. We just need something pretty to look at while we talk business." Mortified, Only Woman remains there for a few minutes, then finally musters the courage to leave the room and go back to her desk, feeling dirty and disgusted. Only Woman packs up her things and leaves, never to set foot in that jobsite trailer again. Nothing happens to Rob. He is promoted six weeks later.

Executive

Only Woman moves on and works her way up over the years to become a VP of HR in the construction industry. Now in her late forties, Executive Woman has twenty years of experience, two master's degrees, and several HR designations. She is the most educated person among the executive ranks in the organization. In spite of her education and experience, she is still fighting against a myth instilled by her bosses that, because she is the only executive woman, she must be fixed to be successful.

Executive Woman and her new male employee, twenty-five-year-old Steven, who has two years of experience, are asked to present human resource metrics at the executive meeting. As she begins to address high turnover statistics, the COO rolls his eyes and starts his inquisition. "Where did you get this data? You must have made it up! Is it complete? Why are you wasting my time?" Executive Woman can't get a word in edgewise to answer.

The COO moves to directing his questions toward Steven. His demeanor changes. "Steven, what do you think about turnover? Is it a problem?" Steven is given the gift of time to respond. The meeting wraps up, and Executive Woman marches straight into her boss's office, declaring, "It is not OK for the COO to belittle me then expect Steven to have all the answers." She wishes for a supportive response—something like, "You are right. Let's change this now!" Instead, she gets what she was expecting—a meager, "You are going to have to learn to not let him get to you." She persists, "Why? Why do I have to learn that? Why doesn't he need to learn to respect me?" Her boss sheepishly replies, "That's just the way it is. Just don't let him get to you!"

From then on, Steven is asked to present at the executive meetings. Executive Woman is no longer invited. When she asks why, her boss responds, "You just stress the COO out. Don't get me wrong, he likes your work; he just likes to hear about it from someone less . . . emotional." The Executive Woman is no longer in the room.

Adult Workplace Bully

It is ignorant and dangerous to think that once people hit the age of adulthood and enter the workplace, they will suddenly have the wisdom and maturity to play nice at work. When faced with conflict and competition, people revert to what they know and what has worked for them in the past. A person who was successful by using bullying behavior on the playground and in school will most likely continue to be a bully at work. Workplace bullying is not illegal and is seldom identified or addressed. Human resource departments provide training on harassment and ethics that may touch on the bullying traits; however, hitting the topic head-on and providing resources that might actually change behavior is virtually absent in corporations today. StopBullying.gov states that the key to solving the bullying crisis impacting our youth is adult intervention.[33] The important question is, Who is going to intervene in the workplace?

The Catalyst for Change

Ruth Namie and her husband, Gary, were among the first to shed light on and attempt to change the epidemic of bullying at work. Unfortunately, their views stemmed from Ruth's own horrific experience of workplace bullying.

Ruth, a clinical psychologist, obtained a job with a large health-care clinic. She was very successful and well liked by her boss, peers, and patients. After a few years, Ruth sought out a new position within the network and selected a clinic for its proximity to home, the neighborhood, and its reputation and work. Ruth forgot one critical point: she did not evaluate her new boss.

Unfortunately, Ruth fell into a trap. Ruth's new boss had worked for the clinic for many years. She had tenure. It was not long before her boss intentionally sabotaged Ruth's ability to perform her job. She denied her access to a computer for more than a month. Coworkers shunned Ruth. They would not invite her to lunch. They never talked to her at the office. Later on, coworkers confided to Ruth that Sheila had warned them not to engage with her, or their jobs would be in jeopardy.

Then Ruth began to hear rumors about her boss's notoriety for creating a toxic work culture, which plagued her department with high turnover. The executives were aware of this hostile environment, but they did nothing about it. The boss was protected. In desperation, Ruth finally filed a report to the EAP (employee assistance plan) counselor, but she never received a response. As time passed, the bullying behavior escalated. She was asked to do needless, tedious assignments, was interrogated in meetings, and, finally, was not allowed to see her clients. Ruth became sick. She was throwing up on the way to work, she lost her appetite, and she could not sleep. Ruth never confided in her husband and never told anyone at work. Ruth was a trained clinical psychologist with a history of helping others. However, in this tense situation, she could not seem to help herself. By the time Ruth finally left, she was diagnosed with posttraumatic stress disorder (PTSD). She pursued litigation, which was an eye-opening experience. Ruth learned that there is actually a thing called an equal opportunity harasser. Being a bad boss is not considered illegal. As long as the bully treats everyone equally, bad behavior is accepted.

Ruth's experience was the catalyst for Gary and Ruth to launch the Workplace Bullying Institute (WorkplaceBullying.org), the most cited authority on workplace bullying in the world. Several key findings of their research include:

- Bullying is either boss to subordinate or peer to peer.
    » Bosses can threaten a target's identity, money, livelihood, family, and insurance benefits.
    » Peer-to-peer bullying occurs when a group targets one person. It is often influenced by the subtle, unspoken expectations of the boss. The peers withhold social support, and the target feels less human and becomes isolated. If the target escalates the situation to a boss, they are typically told to work it out amongst themselves.

- Seventy percent of bullies are male bosses.

- Thirty percent of bullies are women, and 67 percent of time, they target other women.

- Women are known for their natural tendencies of nurturing and compassion. However, as women move up the corporate ladder, they go through a socialization process through which self-preservation and bullying tendencies take over. Nurturing is often left at home.

- The most harmed group in the US is the baby boomer group. They have held on to the notion of loyalty to a company at all costs. They feel a responsibility for their family and commitments and are less likely to leave a toxic environment. They will hold on and blame themselves and be subjected to long-term harm.

- The least likely generation to tolerate bullying in the workplace are the millennials. They don't expect loyalty or security from an employer. They are more likely to leave when trouble begins.

- Executive management regards the bully as too valuable to lose and may provide protection.

- The target is perceived as a troublemaker and may experience more abuse, isolation, or, ultimately, banishment.[34]

Sexual Harassment Is a Form of Bullying

As reported in 2018 in *Engineering News-Record* magazine, a study was conducted on sexual harassment in the construction industry with the goal of identifying issues and developing proactive solutions, and the findings were as expected. Sexual harassment is rampant and continues to plague the industry. More than 1,248 respondents in the architecture, engineering, and construction sectors responded. The respondents had the opportunity to leave personal comments about their own experiences, including:

- "As a high-level engineer in management, I still get patted on the head and told to play nice."

- "Reporting pervasive gender bias is a joke. Nothing is ever done to the offender."
- "Men are on guard when working with a new woman. I dealt with one bad experience quietly because I didn't want other men to be scared to work with me in the future."[35]

As part of a leadership development program, Kaitlyn, a twenty-four-year-old engineer at a large construction firm, was transferred to a new region. She was placed on a project with two project managers who embraced a culture of locker-room talk. At first, she accepted it as a normal part of construction. She thought to herself, *I just need to toughen up.* As time went on, things escalated with one of her bosses. The comments were directed at Kaitlyn. This progressed to her boss touching her. "As he laughed, he would give me a bear hug or ruffle my hair. Even though I asked him not to, he continued. I felt helpless. I told myself, 'If I work harder, he will respect me, and finally this will stop.'" He didn't stop. "It wasn't one horrific event. It was chronic disrespect that degraded my self-confidence and self-worth, both at work and at home."

Coworkers were aware but acted oblivious. Fear stopped Kaitlyn from confiding in her boyfriend. As she isolated herself, she began searching for other opportunities. Finally, she confided in two female coworkers. "It was at that moment I realized what I had been putting up with was not normal and it wasn't right. I decided to report to HR in hopes of improving my situation and preventing this from happening to someone else."

Within one hour of filing her report, Kaitlyn received a call from HR, and the next day, the HR director flew down to meet Kaitlyn and interview the manager. The investigation revealed that the manager had harassed others on the project as well, which led to his termination.

Rumors spread across the company. Kaitlyn experienced an odd mixture of emotions, including relief for finally being free of the situation and guilt for having contributed to the manager's termination. Kaitlyn received mostly positive feedback. A few people assumed Kaitlyn had made the whole thing up. As the months passed, she was transferred to another project with a very positive and safe culture, more representative of the core values of her company. Still, she felt like she had to work even harder to prove herself because of all the rumors.

Kaitlyn's experience led to her company starting the Women in Construction Network, which meets twice a year and brings together women to discuss unique challenges like sexual harassment. By sharing her story, she hopes to educate and empower other women to be better able to take a stand so that everyone can be treated with respect.[36]

Breakthrough

Personal Strategies for Bullying

There are two distinct roles being played throughout our work society: target and bully.

Are You the Target?
If you find yourself a target of bullying, you have four choices.

1. **Bury It:** Denying reality and pretending are coping mechanisms that leaves you clinging to a false sense of perceived reality. When we deny how we truly feel about a situation and bury it, we are ultimately betraying ourselves. In the end, a hostile environment is unsustainable and comes with physical and emotional consequences.

2. **Bear It:** We all have our own unique journeys, which include responsibilities and commitments. Timing plays a role in our

own personal journey, and some of us may be in situations where a paycheck and perceived safety is more important than the risk of change. Before accepting that it is your lot in life to stay in a miserable situation, make sure you revisit your reasoning behind limiting beliefs (chapter 2, "Beliefs") that may be holding you back and actually perpetuating your identity as a target. Working through these limiting beliefs and identifying what is really keeping you in a target situation will lead you to begin planning. A plan is necessary to ensure you feel safe when you finally decide it is time to change. Maybe you will receive a bonus in six months, and it will be worthwhile to bear the situation before you are ready look for something else. Perhaps a childcare situation requires you to stay for a bit longer than you would like. You are making a decision to bear it for a period of time. That decision itself is empowering. It puts you back in the driver's seat. Rather than accepting a bad situation in perpetuity, you are deciding to bear it for a period of time. You can always change your mind and change your date. A plan gives you power, which ultimately leads to courage.

3. **Buckle Up:** Exploring your reasons for bearing a toxic situation may ultimately lead you to a decision to act. Action requires courage, conviction, and the conscious understanding that once you set the wheels in motion to change a situation, it will indeed change. Change starts with a plan. When dealing with a bully boss, the plan includes many steps:

   » Prepare. It is key to have dates, documentation, and specific examples to make your story credible. Generalities lead to confusion and disappointment. Keep a log of issues with dates, times, and witnesses.

   » Ask for help. Confronting the bully is a path to nowhere. Identify the resources and people available to you that can help you.

» Make a business case to the highest-level manager you can that the bully is too expensive to keep. Point out the costs of recruiting, turnover, and absenteeism and the legal costs of keeping a bully in place. Quantify the impact in dollars.

» Once you take action by reporting a bully, it will not be over. You will feel guilt and even shame; furthermore, assuming the outcome at work is in your favor, you will be questioned, rumors will fly, and some people will take a different side than your own.

4. **Bolt:** When dealing with workplace bullying, the best course of action may be to plan an exit strategy. The work environment may be too toxic to embrace and elicit change. Planning an exit strategy and looking for a new job in an environment that suits you may be the best thing for you. If you are compelled to stay, look for other opportunities in different departments.

Deciding to bolt is nothing to be ashamed of. It is one more way to protect yourself by setting boundaries for what you are willing to tolerate. Remember, you are trading precious hours in your life for a paycheck.

Are You the Bully?

As you reflect on your life, do you identify yourself as a bully? It is difficult to admit that we may actually have bullying tendencies. The bullying epidemic in our society stems from envy and power, which lead to fear.

$$E + P = F$$

• **Envy:** Painful or resentful awareness of an advantage enjoyed by another joined with a desire to possess the same advantage. An object of envious notice or feeling.

- **Power:** Possession of control, authority, or influence over others.
- **Fear:** An unpleasant, often strong, emotion caused by anticipation or awareness of danger.

Fear leads to behaviors that create a wall of self-preservation stemming from insecurities and experiences in our past that we prefer others not to know about. When faced with a situation where you find yourself in self-preservation mode, ask yourself:

- What are you afraid of losing?
- What are you trying to hide?
- What are you trying to prove? And to whom?

The moment we put ourselves on a pedestal, we diminish our capacity for influence, which renders our leadership abilities ineffective and out of touch.

Breakthrough for Business

Hopefully, after reading this chapter, people within an organization will be asking what they can do. The simple solution recommended by the Society for Human Resource Management is to create a workplace antibullying policy. They provide a template at SHRM.org.

Unfortunately, creating a culture in which bullying will become obsolete requires much more than a written policy. It requires management committing to a workplace culture in which humble leaders are celebrated and less drama and insecurity are expected. Change requires organizations to build cultures full of liberated leaders, evolving from pride-based leadership to humility-based leadership.

GiANT Worldwide is a group that was created to help organizations change by focusing on culture. The saying "culture eats strategy for breakfast" has never been truer. A company can have a strategic plan and money investors and be highly successful, but without management commitment to creating a liberating culture, bullies and targeting behavior may permeate the organization.

According to the book *The 100X Leader*, leaders define workplace culture.[37] Executives often say they want to change the culture but that the human resource department is not doing its job. Culture cannot be outsourced. It is not up to the HR department to initiate change. Leaders must live the vision, value, and mission, and they must visibly behave as liberators to each other. A company will never be healthier than its number-one team. If the executive team is looking at an unhealthy culture, they are looking at a mirror image of their own tendencies—the strengths and weaknesses of their leadership styles.

An organization that commits to an antibullying policy must have a leadership team at the top that demonstrates, lives, and breathes their commitment. Without that commitment, very little else will have lasting change. If you force people into a culture, you will only get compliance. You will never achieve true engagement. Employee engagement flows downstream, with the current floating just like a river raft. Engagement will only flow through an organization when the team notices visible engagement at the top.

A symptom of a bully culture is how people treat each other at work. As women rise in their responsibilities and positions, they can become threats to others, and people begin to refer to them as the B word of all Bs: bitches. Why is it so common to refer to a strong woman as a bitch? Is it bullying or something else?

Chapter 10
Bitches

> *The woman who does not require validation from anyone is the most feared individual on the planet.*
>
> —Mohadesea Najumi

Bitch:
1. Informal, often offensive, a malicious, spiteful, or overbearing woman.
2. Informal, offensive, used as a generalized term of abuse and disparagement for a woman.
3. Informal: something that is extremely difficult, objectionable, or unpleasant.

A book titled *The B Words* would be woefully incomplete without addressing the most famous B word of all: bitch. When a woman is called a bitch, two distinct points of view emerge. The traditional—perhaps old-fashioned—reaction is to be offended. On the other hand, to a younger generation and in certain work environments, the word can be considered a compliment. The reaction of the woman on the receiving end of "bitch" is definitely influenced by generation and context.

Bad Bitch

In the traditional sense of the word, it's sad but inevitable that a working woman will at one point or another to be called a bitch.

It typically occurs as a woman shifts from the babe role (chapter 4, "Babes") and becomes more confident and knowledgeable in her position. Perhaps it is related to a promotion or a perceived advantage over someone else, like a flexible schedule or a raise. In my case, it happened early and often; as a sensitive, perhaps emotional person, it not only hurt my feelings but shook my confidence, making me question my self-worth and values. One little word had so much power.

As explored in chapter 9 ("Bullies"), name calling and backstabbing are, unfortunately, not confined to the elementary playground and middle school. Bullying is rampant among adults as well. In spite of HR departments, rule books, ethics, and harassment training, hostile behavior still permeates the workplace. Like bullying, calling someone a bitch is gender-neutral behavior; it can come from a man or from a woman. In the male-dominated field of construction, I knew as I rose up the ranks that I was making a few men uncomfortable, and I guess I had expected some form of retribution. What I was not prepared for was other women stabbing me in the back and doing everything they could to set me up for failure.

The New World of Bitch

Suffice it to say that women may now expect to be referred to as a bitch on a frequent and regular basis, and the commenters who do so may be of any gender. It was a common occurrence throughout the past presidential campaign, during which Hillary Clinton was referred to as a bitch so prevalently that T-shirts were made crying, "Trump That Bitch." Our world has been forever changed by the political fodder of daily name calling, but when a woman is caught off guard and is called a bitch, it still packs a painful punch.

Good Bitch!

Just like other inflammatory words from the past, bitch is losing its stigma among the younger generation. Rap lyrics push boundaries, and words that were once considered derogatory and insulting may have lost their impact. On college campuses, sorority sisters affectionately refer to each other as "bitches," and complaining together is known as a "bitch session." Reality star Stassi Schroeder of Bravo TV's *Vanderpump Rules* recently wrote a book called *Next Level Basic: The Definitive Basic Bitch Handbook,* which celebrates basic bitch rights. While the connotation of the word in certain contexts has changed, women of all ages know the difference between fun and degradation. It is all in the delivery.

Amanda's Story

Upon graduating from law school at the age of twenty-five, Amanda worked in a prosecutor's office—one of the toughest state's attorney's offices in the United States. She relays:

> In my field, being called a bitch was actually a compliment. The job was gritty, and all the women I worked with swore like sailors. My husband, who worked in construction, would always say, "A female state's attorney could make a construction worker blush." When my female colleagues and I were together, we all cussed constantly. Outside of our office, we made people uncomfortable. But in our office and especially in the courtroom, being regarded as a bitch was a compliment. The goal in court was to become a pit bull. That meant you were doing your job. It was amazing if you were someone who could rip apart a witness on the stand. We intentionally embodied the proverbial bitch mentality. A male attorney would not have gotten away with

the hostile cross-examination tactics. A jury would find him abusive. But female to female—the gloves were off. I had a case where the defendant's mother was testifying, providing an alibi for her son, who was accused of murdering his girlfriend. The alibi was bogus, and all the evidence pointed toward her son's guilt. Mom's desperate attempt to provide an alibi was his only hope. During cross-examination, I was a total smart-ass and ripped grandma apart, revealing all of her lies. A man would be perceived as cruel and wouldn't be effective in attacking grandma. I was able to get the job done and not be perceived as cruel.

Breakthrough

While the world of language is changing, there are still some things you can do to recover when someone calls you a bitch to your face or, worse, sabotages you behind your back in an attempt to derail your success. Carol Mitchell's book *Breaking through "Bitch"*[38] provides some insight.

When we think of leaders, we have familiar phrases that reinforce the maleness of power and leadership. What we expect of men in our society is virtually identical to what we expect of leaders, so it is easy to confuse leadership and masculinity. An effective leader is admired for his command of situations and for "being a man." Masculinity is consistent with powerful, authoritative leadership. Men demonstrate power physically, financially, and/ or intellectually, and masculine terms are perceived as good while feminine traits are seen as bad.

Women generally fall into three stereotypes that reinforce expectations:

- Nurturer, caretaker, mother.

- Seductress, sexually idealized women, Barbie.
- Saint, pedestal, Mother Teresa.

Feminine traits such as warmth, caretaking, and expressiveness are emphasized and highly valued in society, but they are not associated with leadership and power. When a woman ignores this set of expectations and demonstrates strong, competent leadership, she is often criticized. She is regarded as harsh, abrasive, and aggressive, which may ultimately lead to being labeled a bitch.

Gina was a software executive at a large software company, overseeing one of their biggest customer implementation programs. As the project manager, part of her role was managing the timeline and delivery of customer commitments. The programmer on the project had a history of missing key deadlines. Gina would then hear the wrath of the customers' complaints and have to go back to square one to manage the relationships. As one more critical deadline approached, Gina communicated via phone and email with the programmer, asking him point blank when he planned on delivering the software update. Instead of responding to Gina, the programmer called the division president and complained about Gina's aggressive attitude. To Gina's surprise, the division president called Gina to discuss her attitude. Gina explained to him, "My job is to oversee the project and ensure that we meet our commitments. Wouldn't you agree that the customer commitments come first?" The president responded, "Yes, but I think you really need to calm down. You're being, well . . . kind of bitchy. Don't you know that you will catch more flies with honey?" Rather than reprimanding the programmer for stalling on key deadlines and supporting Gina in her project leadership role, the president allowed poor performance and actually disciplined Gina for doing her job.

Mitchell's twenty years of research shows that it doesn't need to be this way. Women can turn their unique feminine traits into an advantage. According to *Breaking through "Bitch,"* women need to be assertive, driven, and in control while filing smooth the hard edges associated with stereotypical male leadership.

To avoid the brick wall of "bitch," women can draw on three perceived "feminine" traits to achieve big things without ruffling male egos.

- **Collaboration:** According to Alice Eagly, a professor of women's studies at Northwestern University[39], women are naturally more democratic and collaborative than men, and when women do not act collaboratively, they are ineffective. People do not like being ordered around, especially by a woman. Collaboration takes a knack for finding common ground and requires admitting that there is tension and working with another person to resolve it. Women naturally show more empathy than men, and, as a result, can see situations from another's point of view.

- **Transformational Leadership:** Women have a tendency to treat people as individuals and develop personal relationships. In the case of leadership, this translates to a woman naturally becoming a role model, an inspiration. It is much easier to follow a woman who is inspirational than one who is perceived as confrontational.

- **Positive Discipline:** When it comes to discipline, leaders will take a reward approach or a negative punishment approach. Women naturally gravitate toward positive discipline: "How can I help you be successful?" Men tend toward a negative approach: "If you don't do this, I will fire you." By embracing their natural tendency toward positive discipline, women will be more successful in leading people and teams.

At the end of the day, name calling is a symptom of stress, a lack of self-control, and immaturity. The more women are visible in all roles in the workplace, the more women need to support one another and form lasting relationships. Bonds and friendships provide not only support but also opportunities for networking, which is critical to a woman's success. Bonds are where relationships, business deals, and lasting friendships begin. They make life more interesting and rewarding and provide grounded connections on the playground and in the boardroom.

> **Some days are diamonds,**
> **some days are stones.**
>
> —John Denver

Chapter 11
Bonds

> *Creating the strongest bonds is all about creating the open-minded space for people to be who they are versus forcing them to be who we want them to be.*
>
> —Sylvester McNutt III

Bond:
1. Something that binds or restrains.
2. A binding agreement.
3. An adhesive, cementing material, or fusible ingredient that combines, unites, or strengthens.

Bonds are so important to all aspects of our lives. Women's bonds with family, friends, and coworkers help them navigate change and bring purpose, community, and meaning to their lives.

Humans were meant to connect and support each other through life. We were never meant to go it alone. Our new technological world has made the world much smaller, which allows connections via email, text, and social media to be instant and much easier than the old way of sitting down and writing a letter or spending $200 on a one-hour long-distance call. Yet something has been lost along the way. While we now have the ability to get literally millions of "likes" on social media and acceptance is judged by our number of followers, our connections with other humans in real life have often been compromised or lost. The darker side of technology is this disconnect. This new normal allows strangers to hide in a room and lash out at others from behind a cloak of anonymity. It is now common for people to fall in love with a photo and texts from someone they believe to be perfect, only to find out they have been "catfished" and have fallen in love with a made-up persona. Rather than engaging in the world and experiencing the often messy, emotional journeys of real relationships, young people now choose fake relationships on social media. By ducking away from real life, some never learn what it means to love, break up, lose someone, face disappointment, feel loneliness, or face life head on and then get up, dust themselves off, and continue on to live another day.

When we build up walls so high to protect our hearts and egos from rejection, we cut ourselves off from bonds that can span a lifetime or a few days. Both provide stories that become the fabric of our memories and make up our journey to our purpose in life.

What Is a Bond?

As women go through life, we gather people along the way who support our journey, and we form relationships—bonds. Some stay for a season, and some will be with us over the course of our lifetime. Recently, I visited my hometown of El Paso, Texas, and found myself without a place to stay for the evening. I called my friend Karen, whom I have known since we were four years old. I met her at the neighborhood pool in the summer of 1969. She was there with her older sister, who happened to be shorter than she was. At four years old, I said, "Karen, you have to be older because you are taller." She replied, "Nope. One thing has nothing do with the other." I was perplexed then, but the conversation was interrupting a game of Marco Polo, so I let it go. Just like that, we were friends for life.

I arrived at Karen's house that night to find her holding a Swiffer mop and a glass of wine. She was cleaning her already spotless bathroom like a maniac. I laughed. "All this for me?" We stayed up late drinking wine and catching up on family, friendships, and work. We picked up right where we had left off. Sometimes, a year can go by without much contact, but when we are together, it is like we were never apart. That is my definition of a bond. Something that time, space, and troubles simply cannot break.

I had the opportunity to meet Brenda in 2004, when she was working as a safety assistant for an insurance company. She was part of my service team. We immediately connected. She was young, ambitious, and vibrant, and she had a solid work ethic. A few years later, I received a promotion and was looking for my replacement. The job description I posted was for a high-level safety manager with lots of experience and credentials. What I was really looking for was a right-hand person that I could trust, mentor, and train. Brenda called me and asked to be considered for the position. I was hesitant because I knew she did not have the tenure that I was hoping to find. I explained, "Brenda, I think you would be an excellent safety manager someday. Right now, I need someone with more experience to join the team."

Brenda immediately replied, "I may not have the experience yet, but you know my work ethic, and you know we are a good team. I will do everything you ask me to do. I will work harder than anyone else. I am looking for an opportunity to become a true safety professional, and I just need someone like you to believe in me and give me a chance." At that moment, I decided I could not find a better person, and I hired Brenda. It was the best decision I ever made. We worked together for eight years; I taught her everything I knew, and now she teaches me what she knows. When it was time for Brenda to move on to her next opportunity, I supported her 100 percent. We have a bond that spans both our personal and professional lives. I was lucky enough to stand up in her wedding as one of her bridesmaids.

Many have commented that Brenda and I are unique. In the construction world, where there are so few women leaders, we support and respect one another. We have spoken at conferences together and stand out as an example of how women should treat each other at work. Research shows that it is still uncommon for women to support other women in their leadership journeys.[40] In order for things to change, there need to be visible examples of women supporting other women at work. That requires relationship building and networking.

The Difference between Men's and Women's Networking

Men and women network differently and for different reasons. When it comes to promotions, raises, and deals, men's networking groups are more successful than women's groups. This is a result of the intention. Men often have different intentions than women that naturally lead to different outcomes.

When it comes to career advances, deals, raises, and promotions, a study by the Kellogg School of Management[42] of male and female networking groups shows that men's groups provide more benefits to the members than women's groups. Women tend to establish closer relationships with women, while men's networks are more transactional. The difference is not in the group structure; it is in how men and women use the networks that matters.

Women are socialized from elementary school to be nice; girls are nudged away from straightforward and confrontational games in favor of more congenial pastimes like playing house. Certain career experts point out that this gender stereotyping still exists today even though our culture is more enlightened and evolving.[43]

Why Women Need to Network Differently Than Men

Women's Networks	Men's Networks
Interact with women in the same job or at the same level.	Interact with men in higher positions to advance in career.
Formal structure with easy access for women. Men not interested in access.	Informal structure, often based on hobbies (golf, hunting, fishing). Easy for men with similar hobbies to gain access. Difficult for women in similar roles to gain access.
Social structure perceived by women as frivolous, taking time away from family commitments.	Social structure is relatively easy for men to participate in.
Social group attendance may cause perceived conflict in family dynamics.	Social group attendance perceived by family as part of extended job responsibilities.
Women are not comfortable asking for connections if they don't have anything to give back.	Men expect their network to support one another, engage, and provide support for future opportunities and growth.[41]

Women Hesitate to Ask for What They Need

Women have what is referred to as *personal hesitation*. They are less likely to leverage their networks for personal gain. Women tend to undervalue their own worth within a professional network and have a moral concern about using their network if they cannot return the favor in kind. Kelly, a twenty-five-year old marketing coordinator with a small construction firm, joined a women's marketing group. She explained,

I wanted to ask the leader of the group, whom I have a

great relationship with, for a letter of recommendation for a leadership position. I felt awkward because I did not think she knew me well enough to write a letter. I had nothing to offer her, so why would she help me? One day, I finally mustered the courage to ask; she was not only flattered but extremely supportive. We met for coffee, and she reviewed my application, making some great suggestions. By simply asking a question, I got the leadership position and a mentor.

Networking versus Support Group

Women often perceive a networking group as a support group, gravitating toward women at similar levels in organizations and similar roles. Support groups may be comforting and comfortable, but they may not provide the career lift women are expecting.

Support groups do not create access to top-level people in the industry who can provide knowledge, opportunity, and mentoring. It is important to understand the distinction between the two groups and make a decision about where to spend your time. If you are happy in your current position and do not have aspirations of moving up, a support group may serve you perfectly. If your intention is to set up your future for advancement and growth, then a networking group is what you need. Both are amazing. There is no right or wrong choice. In your journey to self-defined success, be confident in what you want and what serves you now. Recognize that it can always change in the future.

Special Circumstances Prevent Networking

Women face special circumstances that can prevent them from networking like men. For example, Jolie, a twenty-six-year-old marketing manager for a fashion line, did not really want to attend events after work because she wanted to get home to be her family. She was the primary caregiver for her two-year-old son. "The last thing I wanted to do after spending the entire day away from my son was pay for a babysitter and go out for work." Women also tend to avoid networking with men in social settings because they don't want their behavior to be misconstrued as personal instead of professional. Sometimes, the best networking goes sour.

Christina is a twenty-four-year-old marketing coordinator. She learned all about the importance of networking in college and in her career. She reached out to a twenty-seven-year-old marketing manager at the social media company she wanted to join.

> David and I were from the same hometown and both moved to Silicon Valley at the same time. I reached out and invited him for coffee. We met several times and discussed our mutual career aspirations. I was professional and focused on work. A few weeks passed, and we met for lunch, where we discussed work opportunities and challenges. After lunch, I received a friend request on social media, and I accepted. That evening, I received a sexy shirtless photo of David. Here I was trying to be as professional as possible, hoping to be taken seriously, and instead I got a chest pic. It was disappointing.

When women enlist men as mentors, the relationship can sometimes be viewed differently by each party and be seen by others as more than just a professional one.

I Hear You Knocking, but You Can't Come In

Many networks, especially in male-dominated fields, are informal and virtually impossible for a woman to get into. It is human nature to socialize with people who are like us, so it is natural that men want to go fishing, hunting, et cetera with men. I have dealt with this my entire career. Many of these events occur on the weekend, and I would personally rather spend time with my family than go golfing with the guys. It was never really an issue for me. If I forced myself to join the weekend golf outing with a group of executives in hopes of making a connection and leapfrogging into management, I would be doing more harm to my career than good. A study confirmed that women who try to network like men to get ahead do not fare very well.[44] They are missing the key ingredient of a close inner circle of women. The study revealed that there is a need for a tight-knit female group that provides critical information on job opportunities and challenges. This may include insider information about advancement opportunities, salaries, and even the best way to respond to interview questions. One of the researchers, Brian Uzzi, explained that women are most concerned about an organization's culture and orientation toward women. The best people to provide that kind of information are other women in the organization. The study confirmed that 77 percent of the highest-achieving women interviewed had strong ties with an inner circle of two to three other women. The research also showed that women who form a strong inner circle with other women who can share career advice are nearly three times more likely to get a better job than women who don't have that support system.

Where Exactly Is the Inner Circle?

With so few women in executive leadership, where can a woman find a female willing to participate in an intimate circle? Women hold only 8 percent of top jobs in major corporations, and barely 15 percent of *Fortune* 500 corporate officers are women. Experienced professional women who want to network with women have a smaller pool of top executives with whom to associate, leading to a smaller universe of connections to jobs, resources, and dealmakers.[45]

Not only are female executives virtually nonexistent, they may actually hesitate to network with other women. Margaret, a forty-eight-year old executive vice president for a large construction company, explains:

> I made it to the top of my organization, and as much as I would like to help other women achieve their career aspirations, I'm so busy protecting my own position, dodging the constant daggers that are being thrown at me, I barely have time to do my job. I have to be excellent. There is no margin for error. I have to be more prepared for every meeting and calculate every move to survive. It is similar to *Game of Thrones.* One day I am fighting the enemy, and the next day I'm fighting alongside someone who tried to sabotage me. If I were to be affiliated with a women's network, it would be career suicide for me. I would become a bigger threat to the male executive team than I already am.

Margaret is not alone. Executive women I interviewed who work in construction, architecture, and engineering all had a similar experience. They all agreed that this toxic situation must be changed, but they were too busy protecting their own success to be able to devote the resources to change it. In other words, it's "every woman for herself."

Is It about Gender or Personality?

The reality is that many people—men and women alike—hate the idea of networking. Introverted people, regardless of gender, will need to make more of an effort than naturally connected extroverts.

Breakthrough

Patti DeNucci, author of *The Intentional Networker*,[46] provides sage advice to everyone on how to cultivate meaningful relationships while forming your network and creating bonds. The key to attracting more valuable business relationships is to be intentional. The following tips from DeNucci's book can help all women recognize the value of networking and become more proficient in the process.

- **Recognize Your People:** In the safety industry, we often talk about people "who get it." You know it when you experience someone who is like-minded and understands the impact you want to make in the industry. These are your people. These are the people you want to find through your networking efforts and develop relationships with over time. Women need to identify the networking events where people can understand, appreciate, and support the unique qualities that they bring to the table.

- **Connections Require Cultivation:** Making the connection is just the beginning. One brief interaction is not enough; follow-through is key. It is important to stay consistent and physically visible. Simply sending out emails blasts is not enough to maintain a relationship. DeNucci explains, "You have to commit to putting regular effort into building and maintaining your most valuable connections and relationships, especially if you expect to earn and maintain visibility, trust, loyalty, business, and referrals."

- **Networking Is Not Attendance:** Networking is a term used when attending events to meet people, make connections, seek opportunities and leads, or get the word out about what you are doing. Here are some mistakes that will lead to failure at networking events:
  » Assuming networking is all about you.
  » Believing networking is about selling.
  » Expecting instant results.
  » Networking sporadically instead of making it part of your ongoing business strategy.
  » Showing up when business is slow.
  » Lacking strategy, purpose, or a plan.

- **Choose to Create Bonds by . . .**
  » being a mindful giver.
  » building relationships first.
  » investing in long-term results.
  » making networking a part of your regular business routine.
  » showing up regularly and consistently.
  » being strategic, proactive, and purposeful.
  » attending events that are a good fit.
  » learning and consistently practicing good networking skills.
  » being open to learning and meeting new people.
  » showing a warm, relaxed attitude.
  » investing in timely and considerate follow-up.

Good networkers are not lucky. Through skill, finesse, and practice, they have mastered the ability to spot, attract, and connect with people they are hoping to meet.

I remember well my first meeting with an exceptional speaker at a conference—the best international speaker I have ever seen. She walked into the room with confidence and grace. She owned the stage, and her presentation style engaged each and every member of the audience. After her presentation, I actually wanted to *be* her. Knowing that was impossible, I settled on meeting this incredible speaker. The amazing woman I met is what I refer to as a "badass" in her chosen profession as a speaker, author, and coach. She is polished, confident, engaging, and kind. In the next chapter, I will explore the qualities of badass status and how every woman can become their own unique version of a badass.

Chapter 12
Badasses

Badass:
1. Chiefly US, informal + sometimes offensive, ready to cause or get into trouble.
2. Mean.
3. Chiefly US, informal + sometimes offensive, of formidable strength or skill.

Women are the conscience of our families, communities, and work environments, and their contributions often go unnoticed. In many cases, women are the last to internalize or ever acknowledge their contributions to the world. By embracing our badass, we claim our contributions and become shining examples for future generations to come.

To achieve self-defined success, you must create a plan, put a stake in the ground for what you want out of life, and go after it. But how? Embracing your badass requires two ingredients. First, you must know yourself. Second, you must know the barriers that are in your way. The only way to know yourself is to enlist some help and take a deep dive into what makes you tick. Most people go through life not really thinking about who they truly are. Embarking on a journey to know yourself will make you stand out. Self-awareness is the key to self-defined success. If you don't know what you want, then how do you know whether you have achieved success? To understand barriers, we need to look at societal cultures and worldviews that may be holding you back.

Sociology

Society has created gender categories and defined a distinction between masculine and feminine. Terms like masculine and feminine are *social* terms,[47] not biological ones, and the roles associated with them stem from the categories defined by society. This is where it gets tricky. Scholars describe genders as cultural constructs. To understand culture, we must look at history.

History

The social terms humans have created have resulted in a lot of baggage that has only a tenuous relationship to biological terms, if it has any connection at all. A male is not necessarily a human with particular biological qualities, such as XY chromosomes, testicles, and testosterone. Rather, he is a person who fits into a slot created by the social order. History has defined masculine roles by assigning them cultural myths, including becoming a provider, engaging in politics, earning the right to vote, or serving in the military.

A female is not simply a human with two X chromosomes, a womb, and plenty of estrogen. She is a member of a predetermined human order. The myth of her society assigns her unique feminine roles, such as setting up a home and having a need for protection from violence, and duties like childcare and obedience.

Societal norms—not biology—define the roles, rights, and duties of men and women, thus creating the meaning of manhood and womanhood. These meanings have varied greatly from one society to another throughout the course of history.

While sex is simple, gender is infinitely complicated. Becoming a man or a woman in societal terms is a complicated and demanding undertaking. Males must prove their masculinity constantly throughout their lives in an endless series of rights and performances. A woman must continually convince herself and others that she is feminine enough. Males are in constant dread of losing their claim to manhood, to the point of sacrificing their own lives to be regarded as "real men."

Patriarchal societies have defined men as superior to women and therefore have educated men to think and act in a masculine way and women to think and act in a feminine way. History also shows that society punishes anyone who deviates or crosses those boundaries. That is finally changing in some contexts but is still the case in many countries and religions. However, many societies value masculine qualities over feminine and have left women with fewer resources for health, education, economic opportunities, political power, and freedom of movement.

Psychology

Today's world is full of all kinds of psychological profiling that can help us understand what makes us who we are based on our personality tendencies, which stem from our societal influences. Steve Cockram founded GiANT Worldwide (GiANTWorldwide. com), an organization that has set out to create liberating leaders across the globe. He believes that the epidemic of problems in the workplace today stems from a lack of leadership and common language. Excellent leaders fight for the highest possible good for all of their team. That is badass.

Cockram and his partner Jeremie Kubicek created a fresh look at personality testing by inventing the Five Voices system, which identifies five core voices: Pioneer, Connector, Creator, Guardian, and Nurturer.[48] You can take the test online for free at 5Voices. com/assessment; it is similar to the Myers-Briggs Type Indicator, but better because it is easy to remember. Each one of us has a predominate voice and dabbles in the others.

I will not go into detail here about all these voices except for one: Nurturer. It is no surprise to find out that 60 percent of women have Nurturer as their strongest voice.

A Nurturer is what you would expect: a champion of people, relational harmony, and values.

1. They are pragmatic realists who ask, "Has this really been thought through?"
2. They take genuine delight in celebrating the achievements of others.
3. They are natural team players.
4. They rarely value the contributions they make.

Cockram devised a great analogy for the role of a woman Nurturer in society. Envision a battleground; it's D-Day on Normandy Beach, with bullets flying and everyone shooting and rushing to fight. Everyone, that is, except the medic. The Nurturer, like the medic, doesn't care about firing back at their enemies or protecting their own interests; they just run headlong into the fire to take care of people and patch them up. Oftentimes, they'll sacrifice themselves to bring healing to the people they care about, whether at home, at work, or in the community. Nurturing women will sacrifice themselves to take care of others. Nurturers make up a large percentage of the population, yet they tend to have the quietest voices because they're too busy tending to others' needs to speak up for themselves.

Nurturers are caregivers and consider the needs of everyone but themselves first. They believe in living a life based on their core values and will defend their values to the end. It is not about profit. It is about people. They understand profit has to be made, but people will usually come before profit when there is a trade-off between the two. Nurturers are quieter voices and will keep their opinions to themselves unless the feel they are in a safe environment. They are selfless; they are more excited to see others succeed than to succeed themselves.

In their personal lives, Nurturers are celebrated. They are considered the best mothers because they are constantly meeting the needs of their children; they keep their families going. In business, Nurturers are often overlooked and relegated to supportive administrative roles. When they take on a position of authority, it typically comes from a need to represent the people in the margins who are unheard. There is no such thing as an arrogant Nurturer.

Why Does All This Matter?

To build a better future, we need to be aware of what has held us back in the past. If not, we will continue to bang our heads against the wall, and change will never be sustainable or lasting.

Since the #MeToo movement, many have questioned why women can't seem to achieve equal pay and why women aren't pushing themselves to new levels of management. Why do we have so many men on boards and leading companies?

The reality is that 60 percent of women are Nurturers, which means their tendency is to not push forward unless people sponsor them, create safe environments, and actually help them move forward. There will always be an imbalance in business unless leaders create an environment where Nurturers can be drawn out. It is our responsibility to empower leaders to actively work to create that environment.

My Own Journey to Badass

I was thirty-seven years old with two kids—two and four years old—and a husband who was working overseas in Malaysia indefinitely, and I had not worked in my field in five years. I had lived overseas for five years, and while I was having babies, I'd studied for my Certified Safety Professional (CSP) credential. I knew that I intended to work again when we moved back to the United States, and I realized that the credentials would help me with the reentry. The owner and president of a construction company where I applied to work was a self-made success. He'd begun his construction business with two other people, and it had grown under his leadership into a thriving multi-million-dollar business. He was one of the best men I ever met because he was authentic, perfectly comfortable with being himself. I initially interviewed with the owner. He immediately asked my age and the ages of my kids, my religion, and how I was going to manage work and my kids—questions that are now illegal. He asked me about my parents, my siblings, and my beliefs. I immediately respected the owner, and we hit it off. I felt comfortable enough to be brutally honest. I explained, "My dream is to work in safety, and I will do everything I can to help you and your company be successful. There is nothing more important than taking care of the workers in the field. For me to do my job well, I need flexibility to raise my kids."

The owner replied, "I think we can work something out. Just come on board, and let's give it a try." And with those simple words, I joined his construction company as their safety and risk manager. The construction industry is a proud one, and many people believed that because I had never worked in construction, I had no business being there. In spite of my experience in safety and risk management in other industries, I was an outsider and a newbie to construction, so people doubted my abilities. The fact that I was a female gave them even more reason to doubt not only me but the owner's decision to hire me. And he never regretted his decision. I had officially achieved the title of badass!

Risk Taking = Badass

A recent study by KPMG[49] that surveyed more than three thousand professional women revealed that less than half (43 percent) were open to taking big risks that are associated with career advancement. A larger number (69 percent) were open to taking small risks to further their careers. The study shows that when it comes to their careers, many women find themselves in a bit of a bind. They are trying to preserve their gains, so instead of playing to win, they're often playing "not to lose" and hesitating to take perceived big risks.

As women get older, their willingness to take risks dissipates. Women with fewer than five years of experience are more willing to take risks compared to those with more than fifteen years' experience—45 percent versus 37 percent. However, the study showed that women understand the rewards that come with the risk. When asked how risk-taking impacted their careers, the responses were as follows:

- "It helped me to be more confident in my abilities" (48 percent).
- "It has allowed me to gain a whole new set of skills" (45 percent).
- "It helped me build respect among my colleagues" (33 percent).
- "It has allowed me to progress more quickly" (28 percent).

Women recognized their aversion to taking big risks was holding them back, but that knowledge did not change their behavior.

Breakthrough

There is no better time for women to seize the wave from the #MeToo and #TimesUp movements. Now is the time to take advantage of the progress other women have made to ultimately make needed change.

Personal Empowerment

Remember, you will never achieve self-defined success if you cannot define what that actually means to you. It requires some self-exploration. Take steps to learn about yourself.

1. Know yourself to lead yourself. Even if you have had a Myers-Briggs test in the past, visit the GiANT Worldwide website at 5voices.com and take the Five Voices Assessment. It is free.

2. If you work for a corporation, your company has a mission, a vision, and a value statement. Taking time to get to know your values and what you want to accomplish with your life is critical to living the life you were meant to live. The world needs your talents, your message, and your contributions. Take time to explore, and write down what self-defined success looks like to you—not to your neighbor, your best friend, or your mother, and not according to what your checkbook currently tells you. What do you want to achieve while you are on this planet for a short period of time?

3. Create a vision board. Cut up magazines or create a collage online by Google searching and clipping photos into a Word document. Print it out and put it where you can see it every morning. People may think this is crazy. Who cares? Wouldn't

you rather aspire to greatness and take action toward a goal than sit and wait for shit to happen to you? Shit may still happen, because, in every single life, there will be ups and downs. You have a better chance of riding more ups and recovering faster from downs when you know yourself and have a plan.

4. Aim high. I have found that when I aim for something big, I always ultimately end up in a better place. There are challenges along the way, and I may not end up where I envisioned I would, but I am always better for the journey. Miley Cyrus was right: it's the climb.

5. Review the chapter on beliefs (chapter 2).

6. Women are the worst at taking care of themselves. We take care of everyone else first. This leads to burn out, stress, and anxiety. You must take steps to take care of yourself as well. Balance (chapter 3) is the key to becoming a badass.

Professional Empowerment

As established by the KPMG study above, as women get older, we become more averse to taking risks. One way to change that is to become more comfortable with risk taking. Here is an easy exercise to help you embrace risk. Think about a time in the past when you took a risk. Perhaps you were full of angst about making the ultimate decision to stay or go, but you finally made a decision and moved forward. Maybe it was accepting or leaving a job, moving for an opportunity, or quitting something that no longer served you. Think about the relief you felt when you finally made the decision and took action. Remind yourself that even if the story did not end with the outcome you expected, it took courage to take action. Celebrate the outcome.

In addition, write your story in a journal or on your phone. When faced with decisions, remind yourself of this story and realize you have everything it takes to change. You just need to tap into courage, evaluate the risk, and make a decision.

Becoming and staying badass will be infinitely easier with support from both men and women. Finding champions to encourage you on your journey to self-defined success can still be a lonely, rocky journey. Breaking down the stigma of nontraditional roles in the workplace will require men and women to support each other and work together for the future, which leads me to the next B: bridges.

Chapter 13
Bridges

When you're weary, feeling small
When tears are in your eyes,
I'll dry them all (all)
I'm on your side, oh,
When times get rough
And friends just can't be found
Like a bridge over troubled water
I will lay me down

—Simon & Garfunkel

Bridge:
1. A structure carrying a pathway or roadway over a depression or obstacle (such as a river).
2. A time, place, or means of connection or transition building.

The word "bridge" reminds me of the amazing Simon & Garfunkel song "Bridge over Troubled Water." The words of the song are on point in describing the daunting journeys women have endured as well as the hope that lies ahead. Women have made great strides in the last decade; for the first time in history, there are signs of lasting and significant change. In spite of the successes of the #MeToo movement and the political wins for women across the country, there is still work to be done, cultures to be created, and relationships to be mended. Women will never achieve their greatest success on their own. Women need their husbands, bosses,

Tricia Kagerer

sons, and friends to be brave, empowered, forward-thinking men who will build bridges over the troubled water that has existed since the Industrial Revolution. It's time for change, and it requires bold leadership.

One bold man has dedicated his life's work to building such bridges and demonstrating how men can truly change and support women today. Jeffery Tobias Halter is the founder of YWomen (YWomen.biz), which focuses on engaging men in women's leadership advancement. The following is Halter's take on the situation and the breakthrough solutions.

Workplace Reality Check

Let's remember that the corporate world was designed by men. It has been a male institution since its inception. Senior leadership is comprised of 85 percent men, who can be 85 percent of the problem or 85 percent of the solution. Long-term systemic transformation will require understanding, leadership, and a will to change. Some of the change initiatives developed by organizations to date have had the best of intentions but have fallen short in making a sustainable difference for women. These include diversity and inclusion (DI) initiatives, to which organizations have devoted time, money, and resources. Yet many men perceive DI as a zero-sum proposition. These disenfranchised men believe that a woman's gain may lead to their own personal loss. Four conditions contribute to the epidemic of disenfranchised men at work:

- **Apathy:** "I don't understand the issue."
- **Empathy:** "I don't understand that women are actually having different experiences than men."
- **Fear:** "I get it, but I may say or do the wrong thing. I will lose my masculinity and status with my male peer group if I speak out."

152

- **Accountability:** "It is not important to my boss or to the leadership of my organization. I don't get paid to support women, so why bother?"

Do Women Really Need to Be Fixed?

Many organizations buy into the myth that the key to retaining women is to "fix" them by sending them to training programs, creating resource groups, or just recruiting more women. Male-dominated industries like construction, oil, gas, and engineering have increased their efforts to attract and retain women by focusing on college-recruitment efforts and creating women's leadership programs. These programs are very important, but they are only one-third of the solution. To achieve gender equity—frankly, to achieve equity for all employees—organizations must address all these issues: (1) developing women's leadership initiatives, (2) operationalizing the business case for women and diversity to ultimately change corporate culture, and (3) creating male organizational advocates. A perfect example of a "fix the women" philosophy can be seen in Kaitlyn's story in chapter 9, "Bullies."

One and Only

McKinsey's *Women in the Workplace 2018* study described how many organizations identify and promote only one woman—referred to as the "Only"—to an executive leadership role and then believe their diversity and inclusion work is complete. One in five women report being an Only at work. This is twice as common for senior-level women and women in technical roles, among whom approximately 40 percent are Onlys.[50]

Onlys have a significantly worse experience than women who work with other women. More than 80 percent are on the receiving end of microaggressions, compared to 64 percent of women as a whole. They are more likely to have their abilities challenged, to be subjected to unprofessional and demeaning remarks, and to feel like they cannot talk about their personal lives at work. Most notably, Onlys are almost twice as likely to have been sexually harassed at some point in their careers.

Onlys stand out in a crowd of men, and the heightened visibility can make them targets for bias. While they are each just one person, they often become a stand-in for all women; their individual successes or failures become a litmus test for what all women are capable of doing. With everyone's eyes on them, Onlys can be heavily scrutinized and held to higher standards. As a result, they most often feel pressure to perform, are put on guard, and are left out.

Being an Only also impacts the way women view their workplace. Compared to other women, Onlys often believe that the best opportunities rarely go to the most deserving employees, promotions are not fair and objective, and ideas are judged by who raised them rather than by their quality. Given the negative experiences and feelings associated with being an Only, Onlys are one and a half times more likely to think about leaving their job. [51]

An Only faces a unique set of circumstances that lead to odd, frustrating work challenges. Marie is a VP of an international construction firm. Throughout the course of her career, she has had too many experiences as an Only to count. Gender bias and misunderstanding come with the territory. For example, after attending an executive retreat with a small group of men, a sixty-three-year-old white male approached her and asked her to get his luggage from the concierge and put it in his car. Confused, she politely responded, "You must have me confused with someone else. I work with you on the executive team."

He responded, "Whatever! If you can't do it, find that girl who should." Even after two days of working side by side, the executive still could not distinguish one woman from another.

A Few Good Men

I have been an Only for far too many years to count. I have more degrees and designations than anyone in the organization, and I have worked extremely hard to get the coveted Only seat at the table. And yet the reality is that none of it would have mattered if it were not for the good men who cracked open the door and gave me a chance. They all had similar qualities. They respected me, treated me as an equal, defended me, and supported me when it was obvious that I was not being supported because of my gender; they gave me a chance to grow and learn within their organizations.

When I was twenty-one years old, I had two degrees from college, and my work experience consisted of sandwich maker, typist, receptionist, and waitress. I applied for a job as a claims adjuster. I wore my grandmother's suit to the interview because I didn't own one. My first boss was the director of an employers' insurance office in Texas. In the '80s, it was OK for interviewers to say things like, "You are too young. Why should I hire you?" I responded, "I just need someone to give me a chance. I should not be penalized because I have two degrees at twenty-one years old. It should show you my work ethic." My interviewer replied, "Anyone with that attitude deserves a chance to become a claims adjuster." And he offered me my first job. I made $17,500 a year, and I was given a company car. I had hit the jackpot. I had made it. To this day, I rely on this boss's example of leadership style in leading my own teams. He set high expectations, was always available for questions and support, and passed on his knowledge. He never micromanaged or concerned himself with time clocks and hours. He had a philosophy to never mess with people's time or money. His team was expected to manage their own time. Pay raises were never promised; they were earned. When someone on the team was not meeting his expectations, he dealt with it head on. His team was high performing and happy.

There are many men who have helped me advance my career throughout my journey, and I am sure there will be more in the future. My goal now is to encourage both men and women to pave the way for the new generation by building bridges. The idea of scarcity—of the zero-sum game, of there not being enough room for everyone—is obsolete and broken. Both men and women need to champion the future and abolish the outdated notion of nontraditional roles in the workplace. People should work where they are best suited and have the skills, work ethic, empathy, and talent to perform. One day, gender will have nothing to do with success.

The Business Case for Diversity: The Epiphany

One of Jeffery Tobias Halter's clients was successful in changing their corporate culture after the president had his own epiphany. This midsized, publicly traded company was a great place to work and seemingly had it all—a great corporate culture, continuous growth, low turnover, and terrific profits. During a meeting with his executive team, the president looked around the boardroom and saw eight white men looking back at him. He said, "Gentlemen, I don't know much about this diversity thing, but as I look around me, I don't think we have any."

This company was already successful, so the need to change had not dawned on the president until that very moment. It would have been easy for him to accept the status quo. Instead, this visionary leader realized they were missing something. That's how simple this diversity thing is—and how hard.

While eight white men at a table can, in fact, be diverse, chances are that most of these men arrived at their positions in the company by thinking, behaving, performing, and acting in a manner very similar to the seven other white men in the room. The president realized that if they all looked, thought, and acted like him, why did he need them at this table? More importantly, he asked himself, "Does the way the executive team thinks and acts represent the mindset of the majority of our employees and customers?" The answer was no, which ultimately was the catalyst for change.

Breakthrough

Creating lasting, sustainable change and building a bridge to the future will take commitment from everyone. Here are some things we can do.

Women: Self-Check

Can you honestly say that you champion other women in the workplace? How do you know for sure? Where are you on the advocacy continuum, and what else could you do to create a more inclusive and diverse workplace? In order to really check where you are in support of other women, take the time to participate in the Gender Advocacy Profile quiz at YWomen.biz/male-advocacy-profile. These twenty questions will help you determine how committed you are to embracing gender equality in workplace dynamics.

Recruit Male Advocates

Most women know "ready now" men who have expressed interest in women's equity topics. Perhaps they are the father of a daughter, had a working mother, or have a working spouse. They are interested in being supportive but just need some direction or ideas on how to parlay their interest into being an ally or acting as an advocate. Women must take the initiative. Invite male colleagues to coffee; set up a call or a meeting, and candidly share your experiences as a woman in the industry or in the organization. Then invite them to attend a women's leadership meeting or program. If your organization does not have one, discuss the option of leading such a group.

Point prospective male advocates in the direction of online tools such as:

- The Male Advocacy Profile (YWomen.biz/male-advocacy-profile), a quiz to assess where a man is on the advocacy spectrum and provide tips for championing the cause.

- The Father of a Daughter Initiative (YWomen.biz/father-of-daughter-initiative), a roadmap to help men make the connection between women at work and their daughters and to take action to bring about change for the women in their lives. Some actions include encouraging qualified women to apply for positions when they become available, mentoring or sponsoring a female coworker, having a candid conversation with a female coworker about her experiences working in the company, and becoming aware of and correcting microbias in the workplace.

Men

Men should start with the Male Advocacy Profile to recognize any unconscious barriers they may have to truly supporting women in the workplace. Today's reality is that some men see the #MeToo movement as male bashing and view women as radical and disruptive. Recognizing barriers and tendencies toward disengagement is key to change.

The next step is to get educated about what women face every day. According to a 2018 study on sexual harassment and assault, two in five women will be exposed to sexual harassment in the workplace,[52] and Pew Researchers found that six in ten women say they have been sexually harassed.[53]

Finally, take a good look around your organization and identify the Onlys. If you have promoted one woman and thought your work was complete, think again. Check in with the Only, and get her perspective on what is holding back true and lasting change within your organization.

Executive Leadership

Organizational leaders must recognize that change starts at the top. CEOs set, demonstrate, communicate, and enforce the core values of the company. If an organization's core value is to empower women through diversity, inclusion, and culture, the CEO will provide visible and vocal commitment and a zero-tolerance policy for harassment or discrimination. This isn't just a memo or a page in a corporate handbook; this is leader-led training with visible management commitment. Executives must consider their commitment to the policy. If one of their key executive team members were implicated in a harassment issue, what would they do?

A. Sweep it under the rug by firing and paying off the victim using binding arbitration?

B. Dismiss or discipline the key executive?

C. Create a smear campaign against the accuser?

The news is full of examples of executives who were protected because they were allegedly too powerful to live without; Harry Weinstein and Matt Lauer come to mind. Today, powerful men fall. Is your executive leadership ready to make change in light of the new world we are living in?

As a result of the #MeToo movement, some male leaders have professed that they can no longer be alone with a woman. This notion is dangerous, dysfunctional, and twisted and will completely derail any progress. CEOs need to state very loudly that they will continue to mentor women, conduct one-on-one meetings with women, and include women in company functions.

Organizations should consider doing the following:

1. Establish a workplace harassment and discrimination policy. The policy must be written, well published, distributed, and visibly supported by leadership. It must be implemented equally across the board, regardless of title, position, power, or profit.

2. Revise or discontinue forced arbitration clauses in employment contracts. These policies are designed to protect the organization and the harasser and potentially punish the victim. When used incorrectly, they can inadvertently keep a harasser employed and perpetuate a problem.

3. Appoint an outside, third-party ombudsperson to oversee this work. In most companies, HR is trained in how to handle various situations, but their charter is to support and protect the organization, not necessarily to help the employee navigate the situation.

Embarking on change and breaking down silos is not for the faint of heart. It requires courage to go against the status quo and speak your truth in a world that may not be ready for it. Building bridges where none exist changes the world. The world will only change for the better when people step up and work together toward change, which leads me to the final B: bravery.

Chapter 14
Bravery

> *It takes courage to grow up and*
> *become who you really are.*
>
> —E. E. Cummings

Bravery:
1. The quality or state of having or showing mental or moral strength to face danger, fear, or difficulty.

To create an authentic life and truly achieve self-defined success requires one final B word: bravery. In the world we live in today, it is brave to write a book on women's leadership and put my voice, opinions, and name out there in the universe. It is brave to run for office, go to work, get an education, start a family, bury a loved one, suffer an illness, marry, divorce, have a child, or travel the world. It is brave to admit insecurities and challenges and get up each and every day and start over again in spite of it all. The world needs more brave men and women.

Steve Cockram, creator of GiANT Worldwide,[54] believes "you can't give what you don't possess."

When embarking on writing a women's leadership book and providing advice on how to create an authentic life, I realized—with a little help from my wise twenty-year-old daughter—that I had some work to do in that area.

At fifty-four years old, I was comfortable. I was not happy, challenged, or making a difference, but I was comfortable. I was anything but a badass. I came home from work each day exhausted and made excuses for not doing anything other than watching TV until I fell asleep. It was much more satisfying for me to engage with characters on Netflix living fake lives than to create a life of my own. I reluctantly rolled out of bed each morning, got ready for work, and rushed through the routine to beat traffic. I made every excuse in the world as to why I did not have the time, patience, or energy to find a new job or make any meaningful change that would stop the repetition and the madness.

The interesting thing about change is that it happens anyway; no matter how long or how tight we hold on to things, change continues to happen. People grow older. Some pass away. Relationships, attitudes, priorities, and environments change.

Commitment to intentionally making life changes of any kind—finding a new job, having a child, starting or breaking up a relationship, moving to a new city, beginning a new hobby, or letting go of a situation that no longer matters—requires courage, conviction, and hard work. These decisions create discomfort and fear of the unknown.

People React to Change the Same Way We React to a Fatal Diagnosis

Elisabeth Kübler-Ross's book *On Death and Dying* explores the five stages of grief:

1. Denial
2. Anger
3. Bargaining
4. Depression
5. Acceptance

In the last stage, people embrace their own mortality or inevitable future (or that of a loved one) or some other tragic event. People dying may precede the survivors in this stage of grief, which typically comes with a calm, retrospective view and a stable condition of emotions.

Right before Kübler-Ross died, she coauthored with David Kessler her final book, *On Grief and Grieving: Finding the Meaning of Grief through the Five Stages of Loss.* In this book, they expanded her model to include any form of personal loss, such as the death of a loved one, the loss of a job or income, a major rejection, the end of a relationship or divorce, drug addiction, incarceration, the onset of disease, an infertility diagnosis, and even some minor losses. People do not go through these stages in a linear fashion.[55] We ebb and flow through them at various times and can experience more than one stage at a time.

While change is one of the only constants in our lives, change triggers such emotions; we grieve the loss of a job or income, divorce, or a major rejection the same way we face a fatal diagnosis. Is it any wonder so many people stay in relationships, jobs, and situations that no longer serve them?

Along my journey to empowerment, I had to take a good hard look at myself and figure out what I had to let go of that was no longer serving me. For *The B Words* to help anyone at all, I had to take time to reflect on Steve Cockram's words and face the fact that I couldn't give what I did not possess.

I had to admit to myself that at fifty-four, in spite of all outward appearances, I was not living my own definition of self-defined success. I was sick and afraid, clinging to an identity that I had once coveted but that no longer served me. I had to let go and make changes.

I sought out counseling so that I could cope with the emotions and fear the last year had drudged up as I faced the thought that I might have cancer and might die sooner than I'd expected. But I stayed in denial and shoved the emotions further and further down into my soul until they finally started to surface, tear by tear, day by day, until the ocean of fear, anxiety, and stress finally broke. I had to give up my comfortable addiction to Netflix escapism and find the energy to reengage with the world. I confronted my inner critic. I faced the doubt that came with my desire to write another book and worked on *The B Words*, fearful all the while of putting these words out into the universe and knowing that once I did, the external critics might validate my inner critic and I might make people angry and ultimately fail.

The B Words is my visible testimony of bravery. It is difficult to write about the ugly situations in the workplace that women experience. Yet if these stories are never told, they will never change. As you explore *The B Words* and work through the recommended breakthroughs, you can set intentional change into motion and help it begin.

Here's to the journey. Hold on tight. Be brave.

Acknowledgments

My grandmother, Peggy Prendergast, and my mother, Pat Connorton, were the strongest women I have ever met. I was blessed with two role models of how to live my life who exuded grace, dignity, resilience, and strength.

Peggy Prendergast emigrated from Ireland in 1930 at the age of thirty. Society considered her poor, but she never thought herself poor any day of her life. She lived to be ninety-five and passed away six weeks before my wedding. She had Parkinson's disease and many other ailments, but they never stopped her from living an independent life until the day she died, including any adventure we could scheme up together. Grandma was always up for anything, be it a trip to Walgreens or a road trip across the country. My companion and my best friend, there was not another person that I enjoyed spending time with more than my grandma. She did not complain. She laughed loudly and often and found humor in the crazy turmoil and struggles of life. She loved her family more than anything. The day she passed away, she was in her favorite chair with a cup of tea sitting on the tray next to her, in her home with her cocker spaniel, Lady, by her side. What a wonderful life. What an example of kindness, strength, and happiness.

Pat Connorton, my mother, was a working mom. A nurse. The challenge and curse with nurses is that they can always pick up another shift to make ends meet. Mom worked many hours and shifts throughout my entire life. Yet there was never a day I did not know that she was there for me and always had my back. Her family was her life. She allowed me to bring in every stray dog I could find while I was growing up, and some stray people as well. Our house was chaotic and loud and full of love.

At seventy-three, my mom was diagnosed with pulmonary fibrosis. The day we found out that it was terminal and she had very little time left, Mom turned to me and said, "What a shame. We were having such a good time." I miss you every day, Mom. My rock, my best friend, my biggest fan. You are still with me, guiding me and watching over me, making sure I still have a good time in spite of the crazy challenges of life.

Frank Connorton, my father, has faced more near-death experiences than most, but at eighty-five, he is still strong and dedicated to his family. Dad helped raise my two kids, which gave me the opportunity to work. While I was working and traveling, he spent his retirement years dropping off and picking up my kids from swim practice, school, choir, and football. To this day, my father knows everything that is going on in my life, provides advice, and sends up prayers on my behalf. He is a shining example of how to keep on going even when his body doesn't work the way it used to and everyday activities have become challenging. Dad, you are one of the good guys. A man who let your wife and daughters be who we wanted to be and celebrated our successes along the way.

Thank you to everyone who shared their personal stories to make *The B Words* a reality and to everyone at Brown Books for your support, expertise, and encouragement. This book is for my children: Tommy and Anneliese. As a little girl, all I wanted was to have a family of my own one day. For years, I thought it would never happen. Until you came along. Where would I be without you? I love you more than you will ever know. Keep making a difference in your little corners of the world.

Notes

1. Abraham H. Maslow, *Motivation and Personality*, ed. Robert Frager, James Fadiman, Cynthia McReynolds, and Ruth Cox, 3rd ed. (Pearson Education, 1987).

2. Abraham H. Maslow, "A Dynamic Theory of Human Motivation," *Understanding Human Motivation* (1943): 26–47, https://doi.org/10.1037/11305-004.

3. Soraya L. Chemaly, *Rage Becomes Her: The Power of Women's Anger* (New York: Atria Books, 2019).

4. Claire Cain Miller, "As Women Take Over a Male-Dominated Field, the Pay Drops," *New York Times*, March 18, 2016, https://www.nytimes.com/2016/03/20/upshot/as-women-take-over-a-male-dominated-field-the-pay-drops.html.

5. Jeanne Shaheen, *Tackling the Gender Gap: What Women Entrepreneurs Need to Thrive*, US Senate Committee on Small Business & Entrepreneurship, 2017, https://www.sbc.senate.gov/public/_cache/files/2/5/25bd7ee9-a37b-4d2b-a91a-8b1ad6f5bd58/536DC6E705BBAD3B555BFA4B60DEA025.sbc-tackling-the-gender-gap.december-2017-final.pdf.

6. *Tackling the Gender Gap.*

7. *Tackling the Gender Gap.*

8. Jeremie Kubicek and Steve Cockram, *The 100X Leader: How to Become Someone Worth Following* (Hoboken, NJ: Wiley, 2019), 24.

9. Marcia Wieder, *Dream Coach Workbook*, Dream Coach University, 2003, 58, https://lionessmagazine.com/wp-content/uploads/woocommerce_uploads/2017/08/DreamCoachWorkbookpdf.pdf.

10. Jeffrey M. Schwartz and Rebecca Gladding, *You Are Not Your Brain: The 4-Step Solution for Changing Bad Habits, Ending Unhealthy Thinking, and Taking Control of Your Life* (New York: Avery, 2012).

11. Sara W. Lazar et al., "Meditation Experience Is Associated with Increased Cortical Thickness," *Neuroreport* 16, no. 17 (November 28, 2005): 1893–1897, https://www.doi.org/10.1097/01.wnr.0000186598.66243.19.

12. Brené Brown, *The Power of Vulnerability: Teaching on Authenticity, Connection & Courage* (Sounds True, 2012), audio CD.

13. Liz Troccie Young, in discussion with the author.

14. Larry Alton, "4 Techniques Successful People Use to Make a Positive First Impression," *Entrepreneur,* February 1, 2017, https://www.entrepreneur.com/article/288412; *Dream Coach Workbook,* 58.

15. Brett McKay and Kate McKay, "The Importance of Eye Contact," The Art of Manliness, February 24, 2019, https://www.artofmanliness.com/articles/eye-contact/.

16. Arthur Joseph, *Vocal Power: Harnessing the Power Within* (San Diego, CA: Jodere Group, 2002).

17. Liam Stack, "U.S. Birthrate Drops 4th Year in a Row, Possibly Echoing the Great Recession," *New York Times,* May 17, 2019, www.nytimes.com/2019/05/17/us/us-birthrate-decrease.html.

18. Megan Leonhardt, "Here's How Much Debt Americans Have at Every Age," CNBC, August 20, 2018, https://www.cnbc.com/2018/08/20/how-much-debt-americans-have-at-every-age.html.

19. "Pay Equity & Discrimination," Institute for Women's Policy Research, www.iwpr.org/issue/employment-education-economic-change/pay-equity-discrimination.

20. Women's Institute for a Secure Retirement, *The Effects of Caregiving* (WISER, 2012), https://www.wiserwomen.org/wp-content/uploads/2019/11/effects-of-caregiving-2012.pdf.

21. "Female Life Expectancy," Global Health Observatory (GHO), World Health Organization, www.who.int/gho/women_and_health/mortality/situation_trends_life_expectancy/en/.

22. "Female Life Expectancy."

23. Jane Marie, "Women's Work," September 24, 2018, in *The Dream*, podcast, 39:10, https://www.stitcher.com/podcast/stitcher/the-dream/e/56394468.

24. David G. Smith, Judith E. Rosenstein, and Margaret C. Nikolov, "The Different Words We Use to Describe Male and Female Leaders," *Harvard Business Review*, May 25, 2018, www.hbr.org/2018/05/the-different-words-we-use-to-describe-male-and-female-leaders.

25. "The Different Words We Use."

26. Sylvana Storey, "Unconscious Bias — Making Millions from Theory," *HuffPost*, updated January 15, 2017, www.huffpost.com/entry/unconscious-bias-making-m_b_8771258.

27. Pragya Agarwal, "Unconscious Bias: How It Affects Us More Than We Know," *Forbes*, December 3, 2018, https://www.forbes.com/sites/pragyaagarwaleurope/2018/12/03/unconscious-bias-how-it-affects-us-more-than-we-know/.

28. Eden King, "Why Subtle Bias Is So Often Worse Than Blatant Discrimination," *Harvard Business Review*, July 13, 2016, www.hbr.org/2016/07/why-subtle-bias-is-so-often-worse-than-blatant-discrimination.

29. Catalyst: Workplaces That Work for Women, 2020, www.catalyst.org.

30. "Strategies to Address Unconscious Bias," Office of Diversity and Outreach, University of California, San Francisco, https://diversity.ucsf.edu/resources/strategies-address-unconscious-bias.

31. "Strategies to Address Unconscious Bias."

32. "Pay Equity & Discrimination."

33. "What You Can Do," StopBullying.gov, US Department of Health and Human Services, www.stopbullying.gov/what-you-can-do/index.html.

34. Workplace Bullying Institute, 2019, www.workplacebullying.org; Dr. Gary Namie, in discussion with the author, October 2018.

35. Debra K. Rubin, Janice L. Tuchman, Mary B. Powers, Eydie Cubarrubia, and Mark Shaw, "The Industry Says 'Us Too.'" *Engineering News-Record*, October 11, 2018.

36. "The Industry Says 'Us Too.'"

37. *The 100X Leader*, 155.

38. Carol Vallone Mitchell, *Breaking through "Bitch": How Women Can Shatter Stereotypes and Lead Fearlessly* (Wayne, NJ: Career Press, Inc., 2015).

39. Hilary Hurd Anyaso, "Do Women Have What It Takes?," *Northwestern Now,* July 13, 2011, https://www.northwestern.edu/newscenter/stories/2011/07/women-leadership-eagly.html.

40. Caroline Castrillon, "Why Women Need to Network Differently Than Men to Get Ahead," *Forbes,* March 10, 2019, www.forbes.com/sites/carolinecastrillon/2019/03/10/why-women-need-to-network-differently-than-men-to-get-ahead/.

41. "Why Women Need to Network Differently."

42. Anna Powers, "Women Need to Network Differently to Advance, New Research Suggests," *Forbes,* March 31, 2019, www.forbes/sites/annapowers/2019/03/31/women-need-to-network-differently-to-advance-new-research-suggests/.

43. Benjamin Kessler, Clarissa Cortland, and Zoe Kinias, "Freeing Women – and Men – from Gender Stereotypes," *Knowledge* (blog), INSEAD, March 8, 2019, https://knowledge.insead.edu/blog/insead-blog/freeing-women-and-men-from-gender-stereotypes-11136.

44. Yang Yang, Nitesh V. Chawla, and Brian Uzzi, "A Network's Gender Composition and Communication Pattern Predict Women's Leadership Success," *Proceedings of the National Academy of Sciences* 116, no. 6 (February 5, 2019): 2033–38, https://doi.org/10.1073/pnas.1721438116.

45. "A Network's Gender Composition."

46. Patti DeNucci, *The Intentional Networker: Attracting Powerful Relationships, Referrals & Results in Business* (Austin, TX: Rosewall Press, 2011); Patti DeNucci, in discussion with the author.

47. Yuval Noah Harari, *Sapiens: A Brief History of Humankind* (New York: Harper Perennial, 2015), 149.

48. Steve Cockram, in discussion with the author.

49. KPMG, *2019 KPMG Women's Leadership Study: Risk, Resilience, Reward,* 2019, https://info.kpmg.us/content/dam/info/en/news-perspectives/pdf/2019/KPMG_Womens_Leadership_Study.pdf.

50. Alexis Krivkovich et al., "Women in the Workplace 2018," McKinsey & Company, October 2018, www.mckinsey.com/featured-insights/gender-equality/women-in-the-workplace-2018.

51. "Women in the Workplace 2018."

52. Stop Street Harassment, *The Facts Behind the #MeToo Movement: A National Study on Sexual Harassment and Assault*, 2018, www.stopstreetharassment.org/our-work/nationalstudy/2018-national-sexual-abuse-report.

53. Nikki Graf, "Sexual Harassment at Work in the Era of #MeToo," Pew Research Center, April 4, 2018, www.pewsocialtrends.org/2018/04/04/sexual-harassment-at-work-in-the-era-of-metoo.

54. GiANT, 2019, www.giantworldwide.com.

55. Elisabeth Kübler-Ross and David Kessler, *On Grief and Grieving: Finding the Meaning of Grief through the Five Stages of Loss* (London: Simon & Schuster, 2014).

About the Author

Tricia Kagerer is the executive vice president of risk management for Jordan Foster Construction, a large construction organization that performs civil, multifamily, and general contracting across Texas. A construction industry expert and speaker on various leadership, risk management, and safety topics, and with degrees in business administration and communication-public relations, Tricia has a special passion for servant leadership and diversity in the workplace.

Over the course of her more than twenty years in a historically male-dominated industry, Tricia has found herself too often in the lonely position of the sole woman in the room. It has become her mission to change that. She hopes *The B Words: 13 Words Every Woman Must Navigate for Success* will serve as a force for change, opening the door for the next generation of women professionals to spark a conversation, utilizing their unique voices to advocate for much-needed change, particularly in nontraditional industries like her own.

Tricia Kagerer is a chartered property casualty underwriter (CPCU), a certified safety professional (CSP), a construction risk insurance specialist (CRIS), an associate in risk management (ARM), associate in claims management (AIC), a licensed Texas claims representative and commercial agent, and a past construction panel arbitrator with AAA.

In her free time, Tricia enjoys skiing and spending time with her two dogs and cat. She and her husband, Marcus, have two grown-up children. They reside in Plano, Texas.